Akoben LLC
364 E. Main Street
Suite 1405
Middletown, DE 19709 USA
www.akobenLLC.org

Ordering Information:

Quantity sales. Special discounts are available on quantity purchases by organizations, school districts, and others. For details, contact Akoben at the address above.

ISBN: 978-1-7336862-0-4

Printed in the United States of America

THE

RESTORATIVE JOURNEY

BOOK ONE
THE THEORY & APPLICATION OF
RESTORATIVE PRACTICES

Malik Muhammad, Ed.D.

Contents

Dedication

For those on the journey to restore others and
themselves along the way

Introduction

"Yesterday is gone. Tomorrow has not yet come. We have only today. Let us begin. " — Mother Teresa

I've always been attracted to broken things. From picking the runt of the litter as my first dog at age three, to my current hobby of refinishing and repurposing aged, wood furniture, I've always loved reimagining and rebuilding new futures for people and things who have been counted out. Looking back, I can see now how this interest ultimately led me to Restorative Practices.

Like restoring old furniture, Restorative Practices is all about healing, reimagining, and rebuilding. It has the ability to transform our families, institutions, and communities by accomplishing three things:

- prioritizing relationships
- centralizing the role of community-building and culture
- providing a framework for us to maintain our sanity, accountability and heart while doing both of the above

But what is Restorative Practices?

We can think of Restorative Practices as a framework for understanding and applying principles to prevent and heal harm and restore relationships.

That might sound academic, but it's worth spending some time on. Let's break down that definition, focusing on a few words at a time:

> "A framework for understanding and applying principles to prevent and heal harm and restore relationships."

When we think of Restorative Practices, we should not think of a cute little packaged program with steps you can follow once and then forget about. While some organizations may present their work in that overly simplistic manner, in reality, the essence of Restorative Practices is much more dynamic:

1. Restorative Practices is, first and foremost, a framework. That is, it is a mental and practical construct to guide our thoughts and actions, and it therefore has its own methodology and principles.

2. Secondly, Restorative Practices teaches and insists on a specific understanding of social relations principles. We will discuss this in greater depth below.

3. Lastly, the emphasis is on applying these principles and practices, with special attention being given to the "s" in practices. We will discuss this in more detail in Part 2.

"A framework for understanding and applying principles to prevent and heal harm and restore relationships"

Restorative Practices is, when applied appropriately, a powerful and proactive approach to building community and promoting understanding and harmony. It does this while allowing for all voices to be heard and differences to exist. One master practitioner and friend, Steve Korr, brilliantly argues that 80 percent of our work in Restorative Practices should be proactive. That is, it should be focused on deepening our relationships and creating space for accountability and support before harm is performed. When we transform our everyday culture to align with the principles and practices outlined in this book, we create environments where folks choose not to harm each other, violate its norms, or break with the positive community. In short, this work is mostly about building a healthy community, improving performance and establishing relationships, not solely a focus on harm.

"A framework for understanding and applying principles to prevent and heal harm and restore relationships"

These are not called "positive practices" or "cute practices." They are called "Restorative" Practices! The fact is, as humans, we will harm others, we will violate norms, and we will engage in wrongdoing. If this were not the case, many of our main institutions and leaders, ranging from human resources departments to deans of discipline to many religions, would be unnecessary! If harm, misunderstandings, mistakes, and wrongdoing are a reality, how do we handle these in a way that maintains our integrity and values? As I'll discuss more in Chapter 1, our current punitive paradigm for facing conflict and wrongdoing is largely ineffective. Restorative Practices offers a way to process harm and move towards healing and restoration.

Therefore, Restorative Practices is a framework for understanding and applying principles to prevent and heal harm and restore relationships.

People and organizations around the globe are using Restorative Practices ranging from prevention-based work to rigorous, interactive Restorative Circles. In "Findings from Schools Implementing Restorative Practices" by Sharon Lewis (2009) and "The Evidence" by Dr. Heather Strong and Lawrence Sherman (2007), the research has shown that when we implement these practices instead of using the common consequence centered paradigm, we see serious and violent incidences decrease.

> "People, even more than things, have to be re-stored, renewed, revived, reclaimed and redeemed; never throw out anyone."
> - Audrey Hepburn

This book is the why and how of Restorative Practices and its application to schools, work, and life. It is designed to be both a compendium to trainings offered by Akoben as well as a standalone primer for the practitioner-scholar.

A Side Note on History

We will not take space in this book to delve into the historical roots of Restorative Practices. However, there are some excellent sources that do this very well, including:

- *The Restorative Practices Handbook* by Ted Wachtel, Josh Wachtel and Bob Costello
- *The Little Book of Restorative Justice* by Howard Zehr
- *The Spiritual Roots of Restorative Justice* by Michael L. Hadley
- *Critical Issues in Restorative Justice* edited by Howard Zehr and Barb Toews
- *Restorative Justice: Ideas, Values, Debates* by Gerry Johnstone

It is important to note that the modern expression of Restorative Practices has its origin in the Restorative Justice movement dating back to the mid-twentieth century. In their pioneering work with offenders and victims in the criminal justice system, progressive practitioners tapped into a stream of practice and principles originally belonging to traditional societies of many continents, particularly Africa and Native America. I personally credit practitioners like Ted Wachtel and Kay Prannis for their hard work in popularizing Restorative Practices since the mid-1970s.

How This Book is Organized

We designed this to be a guidebook for the reader. It is written for the practitioner who is new to Restorative Practices but is interested in learning more about this emerging social science. It is also written for those who doubt the hype around Restorative Practices and see it as a progressive "fad." Lastly, it is written for seasoned veterans interested in revisiting the principles of Restorative Practices from a different perspective, one which explicitly integrates culture, trauma, and a strengths-based approach into the framework.

This book can be used in different ways. It can be referenced as a manual by someone going through our trainings, read and consulted frequently by practitioners, or tackled collectively by small groups.

Regardless of which category you're in, the following design elements will help you easily navigate this book:

- This introduction includes an overview of the main ideas of each chapter.
- Each chapter begins with a quotation relevant to that chapter. This quotation can be a good conversation starter if you are reading this book with a group or a point of reflection if you are reading it alone.
- Critical concepts and phrases are broken down and defined for ease of use and understanding. These definitions are emphasized in the text by boxes and bold fonts.

- Sections titled "Notes from the Journey" describe my own professional and personal journey with Restorative Practices. My story is just one example of how this work can be both challenging and transformative.
- At times there will be "Travel Tips" which provide some quick guidance along the way. Look for this icon.
- Each chapter ends with a section entitled "The Least You Should Know." This highlights key information about the theory and practices covered.

Chapter Overview

Part One of the book covers the theory behind Restorative Practices. We begin with Chapter One, entitled "My Restorative Journey," which outlines my own background running a successful alternative high school and explains how I came to be not just a practitioner but a teacher of Restorative Practices.

Chapter Two, "Two Paradigms," introduces two competing approaches to responding to harm: The Restorative Model and the Punitive Model. We explore the benefits and disadvantages of each model and discuss the Restorative Mindset.

Chapter Three, "The Formula for Change," describes the two key ingredients for change: Connection and Challenge. We look at how to build relationships and learn why those relationships are so important to creating change in individuals and communities.

Chapter Four, "The Amazing Social Discipline Window," introduces a critical framework that allows us to analyze how we use authority to build relationships and repair harm. We'll look at how our tendencies to challenge or connect with people help or hurt us in becoming effective leaders, teachers, managers, and parents.

Chapter Five, "Shame that Hurts, Shame that Helps," describes two types of shame: stigmatizing shame, which is hurtful; and reintegrative shame, which is helpful. We discuss the Compass of Shame, which describes common ways we avoid dealing with shame effectively, and explore why processing shame appropriately is so critical within Restorative Practices.

Part Two of the book moves from theory into practice. It begins with Chapter Six, "Wielding Affective Language." This chapter explores the role of Affective Statements and Restorative Questions in both building relationships and repairing harm.

Chapter Seven, "Circles to Connect and Heal," introduces the most important structure in Restorative Practices: the Circle. We look at the benefits of Circles and provide the basic information you need to begin facilitating Circles.

Part Three offers you opportunities to reflect on the material presented in Parts One and Two. In Chapter Eight, "Excuse Me, but I Have a Question!", we tackle the most common and challenging questions we receive from participants and practitioners regarding this work. This chapter is a helpful reference as you engage in your own Restorative Journey and begin to problem-solve obstacles.

Chapter Nine, "Learning Together: Book Study Group Questions," provides guidance and discussion questions for approaching the book as a collective. Finally, Chapter Ten, "Taking this to the Next Level," challenges you to think beyond the basic principles and applications of Restorative Practices and consider how this work addresses some of our greatest challenges, such as disproportionality, oppression, privilege, and power.

Part One: Theory

"One mind, any weapon."
—Martial arts proverb

"You don't make progress by standing on the sidelines, whimpering and complaining. You make progress by implementing ideas."
—Shirley Chisholm

"Action without thought is empty."
—Kwame Nkrumah

1 My Restorative Journey

"Although circumstances may change in the blink of an eye, people change at a slower pace. Even motivated people who welcome change often encounter stumbling blocks that make transformation more complicated than they'd originally anticipated."
—Amy Morin

"The longest journey is from the head to the heart and back again."
—Native American proverb

It was August of 2012, and I was headed into another school year as the Executive Director of the Parkway Academy Schools in Delaware. Our students arrived at our door after discipline or attendance problems had forced them out of their original schools. In the space of four short years, we had grown to operate three different schools, making us the largest provider of alternative education in the state. Eventually, we would receive the 2013 Exemplary Organization award by our parent company, in addition to achieving highest honors by our oversight boards.

I was proud of our work. We could boast that, overall, 96 percent of our students had improved their behavior, 92 percent had increased their GPA, and 87 percent had increased their school attendance while attending our schools. Those are stellar achievements for any program designed to serve the most challenging and marginalized youth! However, our ultimate goal was to help students return to their original schools, which 70 percent of our students did each year.

Therefore, the real testament was not in how our students did while in our program but, rather, in what happened when they returned to their traditional school environments. Did they return to their old patterns, get in trouble, and have to return to an alternative school or program? Only 1.7 percent of our students did! Let me clarify: More than 98 percent of the students we transitioned forward to their original schools successfully remained there.

According to all available metrics, we were successful in helping to transform these young lives by interrupting their cycles of maladaptive behavior and changing their life trajectories. However, despite the success, I couldn't shake a sense of frustration with myself and our organization. In retrospect, I realize it was because we had two critical problems.

First, we had success without a blueprint. We could boast about our outcomes and awards and leverage these to win additional contracts; however, when asked to speak to other alternative education practitioners about our success, I felt challenged by the abstract and general model I was providing. Sure, our schools reflected many of the powerful elements of successful, non-traditional schools, which I could articulate with ease:

- small learning environments
- low student-to-staff ratios
- multi-disciplinary staff
- diverse staff in all domains (race, ethnicity, language, gender, socioeconomic background, educational levels, disciplines)
- community-based programming
- integrated mental-health supports
- progressive discipline model
- consistent professional development process

However, I felt my team and I lacked the ability to clearly communicate how we pulled all of these pieces together into a successful strategy. To use a sports analogy, we had all of our positions filled and equipped appropriately. However, we sent the team out every play without an articulated game plan (unifying theory). We used our huddles (professional development and team meetings) to discuss how folks were feeling, correct the technical skills, and prepare them again for battle. And through all this, we achieved victory. Yet, in the post-game interview, as the coach, I struggled to explain how we did it and how we would sustain victory. The truth was, my colleagues and I had developed a particular school culture that was more than the sum of its parts. That culture was what made all the pieces move together in harmony to produce a positive outcome. But back then, we didn't yet have the framework to see it. I was working from my instincts—the same instincts that had made me pick the runt of the litter when I was a young boy.

Second, despite our success, we were literally losing our young men, particularly our Black and Latino boys. Between 2008 and 2012, we had lost three young men, between the ages of 16 and 19, to homicide. I had known Ron, Ahkee, and Anthony well. I had laughed with them, grown upset with them at times, disciplined them in moments, and cherished them as members of our school family in Wilmington, Delaware. I spoke at their funerals and freely cried with their families, lamenting my own failure to do more to save their young lives. The fact is that all of these young men were killed by other Black and Latino men. Therefore, any work that we did to support and transform the lives of our boys of color had the positive exponential effect of impacting both the potential victims and perpetrators of violence against them.

By this point in my life, working with young men of color had already become my heart's work. This was partly personal; I am a proud Black man and the father, brother, and son of Black men. Additionally, working with youth, including boys of color, was central to my career as an educator and leader. And working with young men of color was even the focus of my academic pursuits, including the dissertation I wrote as part of earning my Doctorate in Education at the University of Delaware, and also the subject of my upcoming book, *We Can Save Our Boys of Color: Promising Practices from the Field.*

Through my personal, professional, and academic experience, I had become confident and quite successful working with many young men of color who came through our school's doors. But I wanted to do even better. I wasn't satisfied that some kids were still slipping through the cracks. In August of 2012, it was alarmingly clear that we needed a powerful and explicit method to not only clarify what we were doing right, but also perform this work more effectively and quickly to literally save our boys of color.

As life would have it, clarity arrived during a white-water rafting trip on the Kennebec River in Maine. While navigating the rapids with colleagues I'd just met from other operations around the country,

I eventually struck up a conversation with a former judge from Tennessee, Steve Hornsby, whom we affectionately called Judge. At this time, Judge was helping to run a large therapeutic foster care operation in Tennessee, but he continued to support juveniles and probation officers by running Restorative Circles. I was immediately intrigued, and we spent the next three hours on the water, several days in person, and the following weeks via email discussing Restorative Practices. I intuitively knew this was what we were looking for in our alternative schools. And, in fact, without even knowing it, we had the beginnings of it already in place.

When I got back home from that trip, I voraciously read everything I could regarding Restorative Practices. I began weaving restorative language into the culture of our schools and connected with the International Institute for Restorative Practices (IIRP) for more training. Within two months, I led a team of ten staff from multiple schools to Bethlehem, Pennsylvania, where we participated in a week-long IIRP immersion program combining trainings and on-site school visits. Following this, I personally returned within two weeks for another set of trainings, completing my Training of Trainers by December 2012.

From the outside, it may seem strange that I moved so quickly from my first learning experience to becoming a certified trainer. But when I first learned about Restorative Practices, it didn't feel like something new as much as it felt like the articulation of principles and beliefs I had always felt to be true. I knew then that in my sixteen years as a teacher and principal, the policies and culture I'd helped establish had a lot in common with the framework and principles of Restorative Justice. That was what had helped make our schools so successful. And I knew that by learning more about Restorative Practices and further implementing it in our schools, we would finally be able to replicate our success—and reach those few students who we were losing.

Since that time, I have trained thousands of individuals across the world—in schools, faith-based organizations, nonprofits, families and businesses—as part of the IIRP and our company, Akoben LLC. I've also partnered and learned from some amazing practitioners, many of whom you will hear about in this book.

Further, Akoben, a small but mighty organization I began in 2012, is disrupting the field by training individuals and organizations on the harmony between Restorative Practices, Trauma-Informed Care, Cultural Relevancy, and Agency and Assets. To learn more about our trainings, visit www.AkobenLLC.org.

The Least You Should Know

- Whether you are looking to apply Restorative Practices to your home, community, school, or work life, the first step is to be honest about the successes you've had as well as the areas where you want to improve.

- At the school where I worked, my team and I had unknowingly been using many of the principles of Restorative Practices. This helped me quickly embrace Restorative Practices once I learned about it. Don't worry if this isn't the case for you. Change looks different in every school, home, workplace, and community.

- Everyone's journey is different. I encourage you to think about the circumstances, interests, and values that brought you to this book; that is the beginning of your own Restorative Journey.

Travel Notes from the Journey

Imagine for a moment that you knew a young man named Damian who was mad at the world and acting out in ways that appeared to be maladaptive and self-defeating. What if you understood why Damian was so angry? What if your connection and relationship with Damian helped you understand his relationship with the institutions that were supposed to—but failing to—serve and help him? What if you learned of the negative impact of those variables through your connection and relationship with him? You could, then, challenge his thinking around those variables because of your connection and relationship with him. Imagine if you challenged him, at age sixteen, to stop raging internally and acting out externally. Imagine if you challenged him to change the things he could not accept in the world and become an activist. Imagine if you challenged him to change himself and the world. Now, imagine if Damian did change himself, and his name, and many years later wrote a book about helping to positively change others. That is the book you are reading here. I was born with the name Damian, but through hard work and with the support of those who challenged me, I channeled my anger into activism and stepped onto a new path. I took the name Malik to symbolize this rebirth.

2 Two Paradigms

"A person who has been punished is not less inclined to behave in a given way; at best, he learns how to avoid punishment" —B. F. Skinner

One of the first questions trainees ask when encountering this work is "What am I going to be able to do once I leave this training?" They want to learn the takeaways, the hard skills that will help them move the needle in their efforts in schools, work, and life. This is a perfectly valid question, as it speaks to all of our desire to maximize our time and energy towards learning content that will have a high yield in our daily lives. As facilitators, we too want to teach and share that type of content. But this question also belies our common bias towards action and practice. That is, we want skills, techniques, and maybe even tricks if you've got them, that we can use tomorrow—or better yet, this afternoon. Our problems are pressing; otherwise, we wouldn't take our most precious resource, time, to be in the room. Therefore, we desire immediate takeaways that will work right now to improve our most challenging issues and resolve our greatest problems.

Well, to say that this is anchored in the modern Western world's obsession with instant gratification would be too easy. This legitimate question is intricately tied to another issue. We believe that to successfully implement Restorative Practices, most of us require a significant paradigm shift. And with any paradigm shift, the focus on being trained in the skills comes second (if not third or fourth). The first and most important step is understanding and establishing a restorative mindset.

This is a critical prerequisite for effective usage of the restorative skills. In other words, without a restorative mindset, we may not wield these practices effectively. In fact, they may become instruments of perpetuating the same status quo that is currently plaguing us.

A Tale of Two Paradigms

In his classic book *The Seven Habits of Highly Effective People*, Stephen Covey defines a paradigm as a theory or map that shapes how we see the world. He draws on the scientific work of twentieth-century physicist Thomas Kuhn to argue that any significant shift to a new paradigm requires a break from the old paradigm. For example, Covey explains that when Copernicus created a new model of our solar system that put the sun at its center, that created a paradigm shift. No longer were the Earth and its humans at the center of the universe. Today, the progressive shift with marginalized women finding their voice in leadership is, and will be, a break from the paradigm of male-dominated leadership in institutions and society.

> **"We can not solve our problems with the same level of thinking that created them."**
> **–Albert Einstein**

Likewise, we can understand Restorative Practices as a break from an old paradigm.

To understand this, it can be helpful to consider both the current paradigm offered by power-based cultures like those found in the United States and in many European societies, as well as the very different paradigm offered by Restorative Practices, which arises from the values and mindset of a collective-based culture. As you'll see, these are two competing and very different paradigms.

The Punitive Model

We call the first the Punitive Model. This has been the dominant model of discipline and use of authority in many power-based societies (including the United States) for a very long time. With the few exceptions of non-European traditional societies, the status quo around the world can largely be understood through this punitive paradigm. In societies with a punitive paradigm, negative behavior is followed by punishment. We see this in most criminal justice systems, in schools, in workplaces, and in families. Here, the emphasis is on naming, proving, and punishing the person who caused harm, with little or no time spent on understanding why the person behaved as they did, how they can be supported to change their behavior, or what the person harmed needs as a result.

A major advantage of this model is that it is expedient and fairly simple. In fact, it is so simple at times that we don't need to apply much thinking or discernment, just merely implement the code of infractions and punishments as someone else designed it. Additionally, it is grounded in language of fairness and impartiality (despite the data which has overwhelmingly shown that it is not) and is marketed as easy to measure and monitor.

TWO PARADIGMS

Punitive Model
"Power-Based"

Infraction/Crime

causes

HARM

REQUIRES

Severity of Sanction

Restorative Model

"Collective-Based"

Infraction/Crime

causes

HARM

creates

NEEDS

REQUIRES

Repair and Restoration

However, the Punitive Model has serious disadvantages, beginning with the process itself. The process can be broken into two parts: first is the defining of the harm committed, and second is in the handing down of a punishment.

When it comes to defining a harm, we spend a disproportionate amount of our energy on categorizing. Here is what that looks like:

- In schools, we have paragraphs in the code of conduct explaining class disturbance vs. interrupting the learning process, and fighting vs. bullying.

- In the workplace, our annual HIPPA trainings outline, sometimes in painstaking detail, the differences between sexual harassment and inappropriate workplace behavior.

- At home, we create (perhaps only informally) a hierarchy of our kids' disrespectful behaviors (eye-rolling, talking back, missing curfew) that warrant varying levels of punishment.

The point is that, in the Punitive Model, we often devote significant time to defining and ranking various wrongdoings. This is a practice borrowed from the criminal justice system. Sometimes, this results in a set of codes so complicated that it takes advanced degrees to understand them. And almost always, the strict definition of infractions leaves little or no room to consider the specifics of any given case. It leads us to believe that half the work in responding to harm is simply in defining and categorizing it.

Once we believe that we've named the wrongdoing properly, we can then devote the remainder of our energy to determining the severity of the consequence. This is where our next set of problems arise.

Within the context of school, we get down to the important business of determining if the offending student should get a parent phone call, detention, or suspension. If detention is the right path, should it be for thirty minutes or forty-five minutes? If suspension is called for, should it be for one day, or for two, three, or ten days? Should it be in-school or out-of-school?

At work, leaders conclude their investigation with Human Resources and get on with implementing a Corrective Action Plan; issue a verbal, written, or final warning; and might terminate the staff member or even report them to the authorities or licensing bodies.

In our personal lives, once we've concluded who did what, we can also impose our own sanctions. We know what they are and which ones we resort to frequently. As parents, they range from a good ol' fashion lecture to removing privileges and, for some, applying physical consequences. In our close relationships and friendships, lectures, screaming, or the silent treatment seem to do the trick.

What all these have in common is a number of major flaws:

The greatest flaw in the Punitive Model is that it doesn't give much, if any, thought to the harm caused by the infraction. It treats all rule-breaking violations as worthy of punishment, regardless of their actual outcome.

Second, the Punitive Model assumes that the sanction will both change the offender's behavior and satisfy the needs of those harmed by the infraction. Too often, neither is true. For example, a 2005 study by the National Bureau of Justice Statistics found that three-quarters of offenders released from prison were re-arrested within five years. Clearly, prison time did not change those individuals' behaviors. And when it comes to the needs of those harmed, our expectation is that they will feel satisfied by the suffering we have imposed on the person who harmed them. Not only does this not take into account the actual needs of the person harmed (for example, the need for emotional safety or financial support), but it promotes a culture in which "justice" takes the form, essentially, of revenge, which can be damaging both to individuals and to our larger communities.

Third, this punitive response often breaks relationships instead of developing or healing them. As parents, teachers, and supervisors, we end up deciding and/or enforcing punishments, which emphasizes our role wielding power over the person rather than supporting their growth. And usually, the person who's committed harm has no opportunity to make things better for the person they've wronged, which leads to further social disconnection.

~Travel Tip~

When we must give a consequence, let's ask ourselves: "How is this designed to help repair, heal, or restore from the harm done?" If we don't know, then our next question should be: "Why am I doing it then?"

Lastly, our society's conscious and subconscious prejudices based on factors such as race, gender, sexual orientation, disability, mental health, and income levels are reflected in this model, which gives harsher consequences to already marginalized people. The data around this is indisputable. Here are two examples of how bias in the U.S. leads to different disciplinary outcomes in schools and the criminal justice system:

- According to a 2018 report by the Government Accountability Office, Black children, American Indian/Alaska Native children, and children with disabilities receive disproportionate rates of suspension and expulsion in K-12 schools.

- A 2017 report from the United States Sentencing Commission found that when Black men and White men commit similar crimes, Black men receive sentences that are on average 19 percent longer.

Of course, our conscious and subconscious biases also impact outcomes in other contexts:

- The Bureau of Labor Statistics has shown that different professions requiring similar educations and skills pay differently depending on whether men or women hold those jobs. For instance, in 2017, custodians (typically men) earned twenty-two percent more than maids and housekeepers (typically women).
- A 2015 article by economist Matt Parrett in the *Journal of Economic Psychology* found that in the restaurant industry, "attractive" servers earn roughly $1,261 more per year than "unattractive" servers.

Most of us don't want to believe we treat people differently based on their race, ability, gender, attractiveness, or other attributes. However, the data proves otherwise. Given how these biases play out in so many parts of our society, we simply cannot expect our systems of discipline to be any different. Unless we take steps to address it, our discipline systems will continue to mirror our biases and contribute to further injustices.

The Restorative Model

Restorative Practices provides an alternative response to wrongdoing. In the Restorative Model, the infraction is identified, but much more attention is given to who was harmed and in what manner. This is an inclusive perspective, often looking at the infraction's impact on the intended victim and beyond to the wider community.

Travel Notes from the Journey

It was 2009 and I was on the phone with my new executive coach as a part of a "High Potential Leadership" Program for fast track leaders in the national human services organization. I was venting to her about a recent rash of employee issues and explaining my philosophy of "Remind, Reprimand, Remove." It was beautiful in its simplicity. Not only did it communicate a clear path for "progressive" discipline but also my no-nonsense approach to handling people. Besides that, it gave me a simple tool to apply to staff and those we served alike. I was proud of the ideology here but also had begun to understand that something was broken, in me and in the thinking. This came after several grueling sessions with my coach reviewing a 360° evaluation, in which feedback was given by my supervisor, peers, and supervisees. She was supportive but relentless in helping me begin to realize that I was not even thinking about another "R" in my philosophy: relationships. I was personally struggling because I was deeply connected to my team but subscribed to an inherently punitive mindset that was disconnecting. It was the recognition of this need for change that made Restorative Practices so exciting and validating for me when I encountered it.

To do this, we must explore and attempt to understand what needs were created by this harm. There are two sets of needs: the needs of the victim, and the needs of the person who caused harm. For instance, an assault victim may have the real need to feel safe and receive monetary support for their medical bills. In another example, a person who caused harm may have the real need to apologize, express their remorse, or be removed from others for a time period. Here we also explore the function or needs of the wrongdoer which prompted the behavior in the first place.

Lastly, a great emphasis is placed on what actions the wrongdoer and community must do to repair and restore relationships, balance, and peace. These "consequences" should be directly linked to addressing the needs created by the harm of the infraction.

The Restorative Model has great advantages. It is a highly personalized process that can offer different paths of restoration and healing depending on the specific needs of the wrongdoer, victim, and community. Its primary aim is not simply to punish those who commit harm but to heal the relationships impacted by their negative behavior. It asks us to believe in people's ability to change, and it offers us paths to help promote that change when possible. This offers an opportunity not only for real accountability, but also for healing and behavior change on the part of the person who causes harm. It models how we would want our loved ones treated if they caused harm to others.

That being said, the Restorative Model invites its own batch of challenges. First and foremost, the restorative process is hard work and makes no pretenses at quick fixes. If you're looking to engage in this work, you must abandon the hope that you and your community will be restored within a week, or even a month. In addition, this work is people-centered and, therefore, tends to look different based on the needs of those involved. This makes it less attractive to legalistically-oriented systems focused on standardization. Finally, the Restorative Model requires us to believe in the transformative power of people. Restorative Practitioners reject the notion that humans are created once and for all.

Can the two paradigms co-exist? In other words, can we have our feet in both worlds at the same time? Check out this question in Chapter Eight.

The Least You Should Know

- Implementing Restorative Practices requires a paradigm shift away from the current Punitive Model's emphasis on punishment.
- Although the Punitive Model is expedient due to its standardization, it has large drawbacks:
  - o It fails to meet the needs of people who cause harm or who are harmed.
  - o It fails to create meaningful behavior change on the part of people who cause harm.
  - o It breaks relationships rather than healing or strengthening them.
  - o It perpetuates society's conscious and unconscious biases based on race, gender, sexual orientation, disability, mental health, income level, and other factors that can lead to marginalization.
- The Restorative Model has a number of advantages:
  - o It can help meet the needs of both people who cause harm and people who are harmed.
  - o It can lead to real behavior change In the part of wrongdoers.
  - o It can heal and strengthen relationships.
- The Restorative Model is not a quick fix. It requires individualized, non-standard responses to infractions. It also requires a belief that people can change.

3   The Formula for Change

"Change is hard because people overestimate the value of what they have—and underestimate the value of what they may gain by giving that up." —James Belasco and Ralph Stayer (*Flight of the Buffalo*)

"There is nothing more difficult to take in hand, more perilous to conduct, or more uncertain in its success, than to take the lead in the introduction of a new order of things." —Niccolo Machiavelli (*The Prince*)

I love the very idea of change. I love stories, movies, and songs about change. I love it when Sam Cooke sang, "I was born by the river, in a little tent, and just like the river I've been running ever since, it's been a long, long time coming, but I know a change gonna come, oh yes it will." I love that, knowing that change is gonna come. I'm afraid of change at times just like everyone else. But what I love is knowing that change is possible, even probable, for all of us and everything. If we believe and embrace that, then we start focusing our energies to change ourselves, which in turn allows us to help others and transform the structures that need changing.

But where is the starting point for change, whether on the individual or community level? We have found that it lies in a very simple formula:

Connection + Challenge = Change

Let's break this down:

An accepted dynamic in the Restorative Practices world is that human beings change their behavior based on their bonds and relationships. In other words, a key to lasting and meaningful behavioral change lies in connection. If we want a student, coworker, or family member to change their behavior, there are many ways we might try to force that

> "Human beings change their behavior based on their bonds and relationships"

change. We can scare or intimidate them, medicate them, hurt them physically or emotionally, isolate them until they comply, etc. However, we can only truly help them change, and change ourselves in turn, when we connect.

I am, of course, referring to authentic, not superficial, connection. Authentic connection occurs when folks get an opportunity to have voice and bonding, when we get to see the humanity in each other, thus making it much harder to hurt and violate each other. I am talking about the kind of work that we do in Restorative Circles (see Chapter Seven), facing each other to listen and share in the collective understanding of our school, community, workplace, family, or tribe.

Connections Are Key

In our experience working with thousands of people across the U.S. and internationally, we have found that the greatest and most decisive factor in determining the effectiveness of our programs and interventions for lasting and transformative change is the quality of our relationships. In short, when it comes to collective success, relationships are the decisive factor.

Travel Notes from the Journey

In our family, I had defaulted to the rule enforcer, the hammer with our children, while my wife was excellent at tending to the hearts of our family. This not only played well into society's expectations of how fathers and mothers should act but also aligned with our professional roles as school principal and psychologist respectively. As I worked more deeply in Restorative Practices, I came to a painful realization. What dawned on me finally was what might happen to our children if something happened to my wife. My skills at compassionate listening (instead of listening to fix), encouraging their dreams (instead of action planning), and building emotional vocabulary (instead of silent self-reflection) were woefully inept. In other words, my beautiful children might suffer because I wanted to stay comfortable. I was pretty good at using a hammer, so everything looked like a nail. My wife is wonderful at building emotional connections, but I've learned how to improve in these areas, too, for the sake of my family and my own peace of mind.

In the absence of a relationship, we are, at best, guessing at what will have a meaningful impact to transform behavior. What happens when our suspensions don't work on Micah because we just rewarded him with a three-day vacation from a place where he would rather not be anyway? What happens when our written warning doesn't motivate Rachel to work more efficiently because the real issue is that she's being harassed by a colleague? How are you going to handle your nephew Javier after you found marijuana in his room and told him he couldn't go on the family beach trip this weekend, but he'd rather stay home and be with his friends anyway?

It is inside of a deeper relationship with them that we would accomplish at least three things: First, we begin to understand their leverage points. That is, what has meaning to them. Secondly, and more importantly (and less manipulative perhaps), through this relationship, they establish a sense of belonging and connection with us, which makes actions which threaten to disappoint, harm, or lose the relationship much more significant. Third, a deeper relationship offers us the opportunity to better understand the causes of their behavior, which increases the chances that we can help them change it.

Ultimately, if we really want our interventions to affect wrongdoers beyond simple, superficial change, then we must connect with them through a rich relationship.

Relationships Impact Success

Research from the education sector provides a strong concrete example of how relationships matter. John Hattie, in his 2009 work *Visible Learning*, a synthesis of over 800 meta-analyses relating to achievement, found that student-teacher relationships are a determining factor for achievement and performance:

"A classroom's social glue is not just an extra enhancement; it has real academic significance. With a strong 0.72 effect size, student-teacher relationships are in the top 10 of all student achievement factors, and group cohesion and peer influences have a strong 0.53 effect size. Contrast these with the surprisingly low 0.09 effect size for teacher content knowledge."

In other words, when it comes to student achievement, a teacher's relationship with their students was 50 percent more important than a student's peer influences and 800 percent more important than the teacher's own content knowledge. Connection really is the driving force for success.

Psychological research around trauma provides similar conclusions about the importance of connections. According to Eric Jensen in *Engaging Students With Poverty In Mind* (2013), "Social bonding and trust help mitigate the adverse effects of chronic stress by prompting the brain to release oxytocin, a neuropeptide that suppresses the 'classic' stress hormones, such as cortisol."

Support and connection are so powerful that they can even help people heal from the chronic effects of trauma.

The Challenge of Disconnection

The flipside of all this connection is, of course, disconnection. The criminologist Leslie Wilkins offers one take on how disconnection impacts a society: "A society can control effectively only those who perceive themselves to be members of it." Now, I have some trepidation with the use of the word "control" here, because in general, controlling people is unhelpful. But what I appreciate about this idea is that we have a serious responsibility to provide order, stability, and structure for those under our care. And we can't fulfill that responsibility if others don't view themselves as part of our school, workplace, or family community.

Let's consider our typical disciplinary consequences for someone who has done wrong:

Some Common Discipline Consequences

Schools	Community	Workplace	Family
Detention	Social isolation	Verbal warning	Yelling; the blame game
Loss of privileges	Fines and community service	Loss of privileges	Loss of privileges
Suspension	Imprisonment	Corrective action plan	Threats; emotional withholding
Expulsion	Exile	Termination	Divorce; expulsion of children from the home

"If you really want suspensions, community services, and corrective action plans to transform behavior, we must deeply, profoundly, and consistently connect with those who are targets of these procedures."

How effective are any of these for someone who doesn't want to be in your school anyway; for someone who doesn't see themselves a part of your community's tribe; for a staff member who doesn't believe or connect with your organization's mission and culture; or for a spouse or child who feels totally disconnected from the family? What are our consequences for a person who is disconnected from us? They are nothing but validations of their disconnection and continued wedges between us. If you really want suspensions, community services, and corrective action plans to transform behavior, we must deeply, profoundly, and consistently connect with those who are targets of these procedures.

My friends, connection and relationships are the decisive factor.

But How Do We Build Relationships?

The process for building positive relationships is an elusive one at times. What we do know is that the best incubator for developing these relationships—not only between those of us in authority and those who have done harm, but among members of the community as a whole—are environments that build social capital. According to the British Dictionary, social capital is defined as:

The networks of relationships among people who live and work in a particular society, enabling that society to function effectively.

There are three characteristics of an environment that builds social capital:

- Vulnerability
- Structures for authentic dialogue
- Acknowledgement of connection

The starting point for connection is when we unleash the power of our own vulnerability! What we know to be true is that our most challenging students, citizens, family members, and colleagues are very effective in using their behavioral vocabulary but struggle with using their emotional vocabulary. I'm arguing that we develop these connections by reaching out to them first, being human with them first, being vulnerable with them first.

Let's revisit my earlier example of Micah, the student who's been suspended from a school he doesn't feel connected to. As a principal, I remember sitting in front of a "Micah" in my office. He was about to be suspended for the third time that month. I told him, "Man, I feel like a failure as your principal because I haven't figured out how to help you." I was being genuine and vulnerable. It was hard to say, but harder for him to hear. He got it. He realized that what was going on here between us mattered to me, was weighing on me. He mattered to me. He finished that year and I never had to say that to him again. My vulnerability helped him understand that, through me, he was connected to the school.

We also build social capital and relationships by creating structures for authentic dialogue. Let's be honest: too often our conversations lack depth and real connection to what matters most. This is especially true in most workplace settings. As such, we miss opportunities to speak our truth and honestly confront our challenges in being together.

Let's think back to my earlier workplace example, where Rachel was performing poorly because of harassment she was facing. Imagine if Rachel had a structure that was a safe space to raise the impact of that harassment. What if the team meeting was a circle process built to not only support and hold staff accountable to performance, but also connect them as humans who were encouraged to be open, authentic, and valued? Rachel could then belong to a community that recognizes her drop in performance as the outcome of an issue rather than the cause of a reprimand. We will discuss Restorative Circles in Chapter Seven.

Lastly, relationships are developed when we acknowledge that we are connected. I know that it sounds obvious, but we don't always realize that we belong to a dyad, triad, or collective. Sometimes it takes awareness or reminding to help us understand that we have rights and responsibilities to others. In our imagined scenario about the teenage Javier and his family's discovery of weed in his room, Javier doesn't realize how important he is to the family and how hard they are working to provide him with a safe and supportive home. By using weed and by keeping it in the family home, he might have jeopardized those in the household with him. He might also have jeopardized the future they are working hard to help him build. But banning him from the beach trip when he'd rather be with his friends anyway doesn't help fix this. We build social capital when we remind Javier that he is of and with this collective. And within that collective, he has rights (to be supported, and to be included as part of the family in events like the beach vacation) and responsibilities (to obey the law, and to respect the work of his family to support him).

We will explore some concrete practices for building relationships in greater detail in Chapter Six: Wielding Affective Language.

Challenge

It is through powerful connections and relationships that we earn the ability to challenge behavior and challenge mindsets. The currency we earn through connection should be used to challenge. A significant benefit of a real relationship is that we get to call BS when necessary. It is inside of this connection that others can hear our voices of disappointment, frustration, and shame.

In my own youth, certain adults in a significant relationship with me used our connection to powerfully challenge me. I heard and felt them when they said, "You carry the hopes and dreams of your family on your shoulders. You tell me that you want to be the first in your family to go to college. How does this drinking and getting high align with that plan?" Or, one of the most impactful was, "Do you have the courage to be more and do more than what you have lived through already?" These folks asked—no, demanded—more of me than anyone else did. They could say and do things that pushed me deeper because our connection was deeper. They took the time not just to point out my disruptive behavior, but to listen to my dreams and goals, then hold me accountable to them.

Change Agents Must Be Assertive

As agents of change, we have a moral obligation to be assertive. We have a responsibility to expect those we serve to

- participate in building a positive community
- be allies in challenging each other's behavior

In their fantastic book *Rules for Revolutionaries: How Big Organizing Can Change Everything*, authors Becky Bond and Zack Exley make a strong case for empowering and holding accountable those you are serving. In Chapter Seven, entitled "The Revolution Will Be Funded – By Small Donations," they challenge the reader to "not become part of the nonprofit industrial complex by claiming to be helping people who care about you so little that they won't pitch in a few bucks to support your work." In other words, charity and big philanthropy must not abdicate the responsibilities of those being served themselves. As change agents, we must push, pull, and challenge the people we serve to always step up and participate, through their own sweat equity, in building a positive community. And as change agents, we must also make sure that we are showing up as valuable members of the community we are serving. To use restorative language, invite them to sit in your circle, but more importantly, find ways to join theirs.

Over time, I have come to appreciate the critical role of peer allies. Perhaps the lesson has been long in coming because of my own overestimation of my range of control. Or perhaps it's my ego or a reluctance to seek help. But if I really believe in the power of connection, then it requires me to identify, recruit, and support allies from among those I'm serving. Not only to share the weight of creating change in general, but specifically to challenge peers in relationships with them so the challenge does not come only from authority figures. I need to help build the capacity of these allies—colleagues, youth, family members, neighbors—to challenge the harm and wrongdoing they witness themselves. It is not too wild of an idea, actually. Men should positively but powerfully challenge their male colleagues and friends when witnessing misogyny. Team members should respectfully but seriously challenge their coworker when witnessing unethical performance. Youth should lovingly but directly address a friend who constantly disrupts math class. As change agents, we should proactively and continuously encourage our allies to hold themselves and others accountable.

Put Training Wheels on it

I remember vividly teaching my daughter how to ride a bike. She has always been an overachiever and independent, just like her Mama and a long line of women in our family tribe, so I knew this was going to be interesting. She was about five, and this was a big deal. Her little brother had just been born, and this was a chance for me to give her some special attention. Behind our Baltimore home was a nice flat alley with few cars; it was the perfect practice spot. Once she got fully outfitted in her protective gear (a fundamental requirement of her Mama), she came outside to "help" me attach the training wheels onto her new bike. Always the inquisitive one, she asked what the training wheels were for, and I explained that they would help her balance the bike.

That first lesson was rough. So were the second through seventh. But at some point, her grip on the handlebars was less shaky, she started looking ahead instead of down at the bike, and she could speak with more confidence instead of screaming "whoa Baba, whoa!" Finally the day came when she was ready. I gave her the wrench and held my hand over hers to help her remove the training wheels. The process of learning to ride started all over but took a lot less time. Her experience with the training wheels had taught her it was going to be tough, but she knew we were going to stay at it until she was victorious. One day I was jogging beside her with a support hand on her handlebars, and it seemed like only a moment later I was calling from a distance to remind her to use her brakes. She got it, and she successfully faced the increasing levels of challenge in riding a bike, all thanks to training wheels.

We can use the same idea with any challenge. "Putting training wheels on it" means to provide supports, but not fully remove the challenge. Training wheels are helpful, sometimes essential, and almost always temporary. They remind us that this work of change is a journey, not a destination. And they allow us to break up a challenge into manageable pieces, helping us see our forward progress along the way.

It's important to note that training wheels are not how we "try" to do something. My daughter was not "trying" to ride a bike; she was actually riding the bike with the support of the training wheels. She was challenged, learned, succeeded, then challenged more.

Change

When we teach, do social work, raise a family, work in a prison, volunteer in our communities, or lead an organization, we are in the business of changing and improving the human condition.

We become better, both individually and collectively, when we leverage our connections with others to challenge them to change. Unfortunately, if we do not challenge each other and ourselves, call BS when appropriate, and hold people accountable, we risk creating an atmosphere of dependency and self-defeat.

This change can only be accomplished once we connect with others through relationships and humanity, then challenge ourselves and them consistently. Here is the formula: CONNECTION + CHALLENGE = CHANGE. The formula is simple, but the work is hard!

The Least You Should Know

- Change happens as a result of connections. When you connect with someone, you can then challenge them to change. The formula is simple: Connection + Challenge = Change.

- Relationships are powerful. For example, studies have shown that when it comes to student achievement, the student-teacher relationship is eight times more important than the teacher's own content knowledge.

- To create connection, we must build social capital. Social capital is the degree of connections among people in a particular community which enable it to function positively and effectively.

- Once a person feels connected to us, we can challenge them to change. Connection allows them to hear our voices of disappointment, frustration, and shame.

CONNECTION + CHALLENGE = CHANGE

4   The Amazing Social Discipline Window

"If civilization is to survive, we must cultivate the science of human
relationships—the ability of all peoples, of all kinds, to live together,
in the same world at peace." —Franklin D. Roosevelt

"I define connection as the energy that exists between people when
they feel seen, heard, and valued; when they can give and receive
without judgment; and when they derive sustenance and strength
from the relationship." —Dr. Brene Brown

The principle of challenging others in order to create change raises
questions about how we use our authority. This is arguably the most
important question when thinking about Restorative Practices.
It informs our collective analysis and self-reflection on how we
are serving others by building social capital on the one hand and
effectively responding to wrongdoing on the other. Restorative
Practices provides a powerful framework through which we can
analyze the use of authority both to build relationships and repair
harm. This framework is called the Social Discipline Window.

Undoubtedly, the most fundamental and radical shift that we can enact as leaders and concerned community members is to transform our use of authority in business, schools, law enforcement, service agencies, families, and the community. Too often, our youth, marginalized communities, and team members do not feel connected to, valued, or uplifted by the institutions and organizations set up to serve and support them. This schism creates the space for both "anti-social" behavior and subsequent punishments in the punitive paradigm. Most often, those punishments serve only to further disconnect people from their communities, deepening the underlying disconnection that made their negative behavior possible to begin with. And so the cycle of punishment ➤ disconnectedness ➤ negative behavior ➤ punishment replicates itself throughout the tenure of that relationship.

According to Ted Wachtel, founder of the International Institute for Restorative Practices, people are "happier, more cooperative and productive, and more likely to make positive changes in their behavior when those in positions of authority do things with them, rather than to them or for them." When my colleagues and I share this statement with people in workshops, they nod their heads intuitively. It is simple yet profound, like all great ideas which take root in our hearts and work.

Social Discipline Window

One of the most powerful frameworks that we use in Restorative Practices is the Social Discipline Window. This simple two-by-two matrix provides a tool of analysis that can flow from the superficial to the profound in understanding our use of authority. The Social Discipline Window was developed by Ted Wachtel and the International Institute for Restorative Practices (www.iirp.edu). This brilliant framework is unquestionably the most important element of our training material, as well as my personal favorite piece to teach. I

love and appreciate how simple it is, yet it has layers that we unpack together to deepen understanding and self-reflection.

Based on our work in Akoben, I have modified the language in the original Social Discipline Window to reflect the "Formula for Change" as described in the last chapter. I see this as a natural progression of this important framework.

In the simplest of terms, we can understand authority as being in the intersection of both challenge and connection:

- Challenge refers to setting limits, establishing expectations, providing structure, holding folks accountable, and providing norms and standards.
- Connection refers to being nurturing; being compassionate; and wielding empathy, connection, and love.

In the Social Discipline Window graphic below, the quadrants reflect the intersection and degree of challenge and connection in our use of authority.

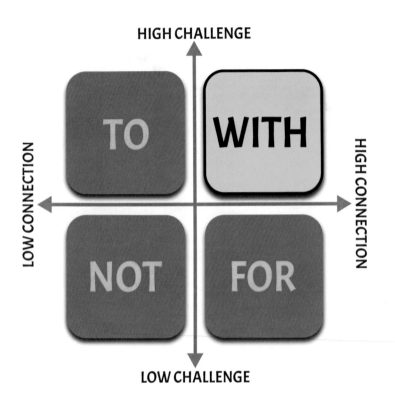

HIGH CHALLENGE

LOW CONNECTION

TO WITH

NOT FOR

HIGH CONNECTION

LOW CHALLENGE

The NOT Box

We can start in the lower left-hand quadrant, which reflects a use of authority that is both low in challenge and low in connection. The leader, teacher, police officer, community worker, or parent who operates in this box has made a choice to abdicate their responsibility either to set limits or provide compassion for those under their care. In their presence, people are given either expressed or indirect permission to act in any way they choose without someone correcting or addressing their behavior, providing guidance, or intervening with appropriate strength and seriousness. Additionally, they are clear that this disengagement is not centered in love or compassion, but rather in the natural distancing created when faced with things you ignore. Therefore, we refer to this as the NOT box. The adults that are operating here are NOT engaged, NOT effective, and, in effect, NOT really present.

The TO Box

The upper left-hand quadrant represents the use of authority that is high in challenge and low in connection. This space is most commonly accessed by the authoritarian, dictator, or heavy handed administrator—in short, the tough principal Joe Clark as depicted in the movie *Lean on Me*. Sayings like "it's my way or the highway," "these folks have to learn the hard way—we can't baby them," and "I'm not here to like you, I'm here to teach/lead/police you" are often used by these folks to justify their excessive fixation with control. The actions of this approach are often coated in language of self-determination like "I'm just preparing our young people for a challenging world" or "My leadership is about providing much-needed structure and order." In fact, this use of authority finds value only in accountability, compliance, and obedience. There is little interest in emotional intelligence or developing an internal locus of control within those they serve. In fact, when unchecked or at its extreme, this approach is just about control.

At face value, this approach can move the needle on the metrics the leader finds most valuable (e.g. law and order, tests, safety, profit). However, there is no authentic relationship of respect between both parties, and when the leader is away, people have no internally driven motivation.

Travel Notes from the Journey

I sought leadership, power, and influence at a young age. My first formal leadership position came when I was fifteen and elected as the first president of the Minority Youth Educational Institute (MYEI), a partnership between Gettysburg College and the local Gettysburg, Pennsylvania community. Since then, I have had the honor to hold many positions, including some where I shined and a few where I certainly did not. Regardless of the position, I always felt lonely and frustrated by what I perceived as the lack of a bench of other leaders in the group who would step up when necessary. In reality, however, now I can see that my leadership style was probably standing in the way of others' finding their own space and opportunities to step up. My own TO approach and perception was an impediment to the very thing I said that I wanted. By reflecting on the Social Discipline Window framework, I've been encouraged to find more and more ways to simmer down, create space, and nudge those I serve and serve with into their own leadership moments.

The FOR Box

The lower right-hand quadrant appears to be the polar opposite of the TO box in that it represents high connection and low challenge. Here resides the leader, teacher, community worker, or parent who acts with their heart and cherishes friendships with those they serve. They also operate from a deficiency mindset cloaked in praise and hugs. Excuses, background, and disabilities are all accepted and cited by them to underscore why they (and the rest of us) should carry much of the weight and not hold others accountable. Like their TO counterparts, the needle on some metrics can move; however, we see a normalization of negative behavior and frustration once the pizza, immediate attention, or other external rewards run out. We refer to this quadrant as the FOR box. The leaders operating here use their authority to do things FOR those they serve. When unchecked or at its extreme this approach is just about providing support.

The WITH Box

The upper right-hand quadrant represents the polar opposite of the NOT box. It is the quadrant of full engagement through a blend of high challenge and high connection. This is the environment where you set clear limits and direction, hold others accountable, nurture their authentic personalities, listen to their voices, and respect their needs. This is the space where the restorative practitioner operates, as do most effective leaders, educators, parents, and team members. However, it requires conscious effort because none of us naturally exists within this quadrant. It takes work and effort to build our skills and comfort level to arrive at this point. Usually, when we think of our idols, they exemplify this balance between challenge and connection. Their high challenge is rooted in the highest of expectations and in believing in our potential. Their high connection is often rooted in unconditional love. We call this the WITH box since those who operate here engage, collaborate, and do things WITH those they serve.

Our use of authority and which quadrant we operate in most often is influenced by a host of factors, including our own backgrounds; emotional scripting around needs for power, control, and acceptance; and a sense of burnout. After implementing this work across the U.S. and internationally, my colleagues and I have seen that most of us fluctuate in our use of authority between the TO and FOR boxes. In reality, this often has very little to do with meeting the needs of those we serve and more to do with what is going on with us personally. However, our decisions while in the TO, FOR, NOT, and WITH boxes can (and always do) have an effect on those we serve and ripple out to impact families, the community, and stakeholders. Therefore, it's crucial that we learn to operate with their needs in mind.

"You don't need to cede control of your class, or even offer students particularly significant choices. The feeling of having some control is at least as important as actually having control."
–Eric Jensen

The Social Discipline Window in Practice

In our trainings around Restorative Practices, I have never had a participant admit that they primarily operate in the NOT box. While some may operate with this approach, the twin pressures of shame and self-preservation prevent them from admitting it.

However, while engaged in this work, we have encountered many participants who describe leaders who very much emulate NOT box characteristics. Not surprisingly, youth often see leaders, parents, and teachers who operate in the FOR and WITH boxes as caring and can even interpret the TO's behavior as a manifestation of care and concern. However, for those in the NOT box, the depersonalization and non-engagement that they project communicates a clear message: they do not care about those they are serving. Sometimes, this approach is rooted in a belief that those they are responsible for serving are not worthy of their attention and best efforts. Other times, it is simply a result of fatigue and an underlying feeling that their participation in their organization is a matter of obligation, not preference; therefore, they will offer enough minimal effort to remain employed.

To use Stephen Covey's terms, this is the box of Lose-Lose. The leader loses by using an approach that they know is ineffective and disengaging. If we accept the premise that everyone wants to be successful, then operating in the NOT box represents the self-inflicting pain of hitting your head against the same wall over and over. Those under the authority of the NOT box leader also lose because they have an absentee landlord in place of a responsible, interactive leader.

Whereas the NOT box ignores the value and needs of those being served, the TO and FOR boxes see them from lenses clouded by the leader's own biases. The TO box operates from the dominant societal mindset that people need to be controlled in order to get things done. Not only is the TO box disempowering to those under it, but this is precisely the box where most of our enduring challenges reside. This is the box of mass incarceration where criminal justice systems direct their weapons and policies towards marginalized populations. This is the box of discipline disproportionality where schools do the same thing. This is the box of community violence, where it is more appropriate to exert force of will through violence and control than through connection and cooperation. This is the box of abuse where we "spare the rod and spoil the child" or we encourage uncritical obedience to adults or leaders unwilling or unable to explain themselves (e.g. "because I said so!").

Perhaps more subtle, but also damaging, is the FOR box. When leaders behave with only connection and refuse to establish norms and accountability, they are also manifesting a deficiency mindset. In this style of engagement, leaders won't set high standards, or any standards at all, because they believe recipients are incapable of meeting them. They won't push and apply pressure because they believe the answers lie solely within themselves.

Unfortunately, dependency is the most natural outcome of this kind of engagement. When people are not required to carry any of the weight of their own responsibilities, then their naturally strong shoulders become atrophied. They grow accustomed to leaders providing answers to the hardest problems if they just wait it out. They grow comfortable with bosses giving them a pass on arriving late to work or missing assignments. They come to expect that their parents will accept (and even provide) their excuses for why they behaved in a negative way. A manipulative mindset develops as an outcome of this dependency. If we treat people as though they should be coddled and pitied, they learn that they should and can get us to do things for them. Our own manipulation, cajoling, pleading, and bribing them into behaving (or at least liking us) teaches them that these are acceptable ways to use authority and manage behavior.

Lastly, the FOR quadrant depletes motivation and saps the drive to push on through difficulty. It weakens the fighting capacity and sense of authentic achievement. For instance, it is kind to reassure our youth that they can become anything, but if we don't have them carry the weight of anything, then what will they become? Without the internal fortitude to accept both help and responsibility then they will rise no further than our low expectations of them.

Another expression I love that conveys the dangers of the FOR box comes "surprisingly, for me" from George W. Bush. In a speech he gave in 2000, then-President Bush spoke of the dangers of "another form of bias: the soft bigotry of low expectations." Of course, this type of bigotry is the opposite of what most people in the FOR box intend.

> ❝Accolades preceding effort is self-defeating and dependency creating.❞
>
> –Mwalimu Bomani Baruti

Motivations for each box

Different factors or motivations may move people into certain windows. The following table highlights a few of these for the TO, FOR and NOT boxes.

BOX	Personal Factors	Systemic Factors
TO	• Need for power and control • Feeds ego - Controller • Feeling personally powerless	• Control is valued by the culture • Time constraints • Pressure to perform/high stakes
FOR	• Wanting to make the pain go away • Lack of faith in others • Feeds ego – Savior Syndrome	• Environmental challenges for those you serve (poverty, disability, etc) • Time constraints (easier/faster to do it myself)
NOT	• Lack of skills/competence • Feeling overwhelmed, uncertain, scared, tired	• Environment of learned helplessness • Culture of intimidation

These concepts are critically important for us to understand in order to apply a restorative lens to both ourselves and those we work with, live with, and serve.

In my own Restorative Journey, I have been plagued with challenging my own default TO mindset when thinking about (and judging) folks who might be in the FOR and NOT boxes. I've especially been critical of colleagues operating in the NOT box, making strong judgments like "they are unworthy of their positions" or "they need to get out of the way." However, I'm blessed with some restorative warriors in my tribe like my colleague Steve Korr, a dear friend and brother.

He regularly challenges me to see my own motivations and possibly those of the folks I'm criticizing. In a blog post for Akoben, he wrote:

> Just like very few people are naturally restorative, I also believe that very few people (if any) are naturally in the "NOT" box. Australian criminologist John Braithwaite's research tells us that being in right relationship with others motivates people. We want to be well liked and well thought of. If this is the case, then being in the "NOT" box doesn't make any sense. This way of being ultimately pushes people away and leaves the individual isolated. However, all behaviors serve a need, so what could a person operating in this box be experiencing? Although this is a very deep issue, in my consulting practice I have discovered three main reasons or motivations:
> - being physically and emotionally drained or exhausted
> - feeling lost, overwhelmed or depressed
> - being afraid or fearful
>
> (https://akobenllc.org/not-box-happens/)

Steve has helped me think about people in the NOT box so I can understand their needs and, when appropriate, find ways to help them change. This insight is allowing me to shift my approach from one of judgment to one of hopeful action. And that shift is precisely what Restorative Practices asks of us all.

It is important to remember that the boxes in the Social Discipline Window are general observable tendencies and not permanent states of being. In other words, none of us remains in a single box all the time. We, as human beings, are far more complex than that. Let's use the framework to help understand our state of mind and effectiveness of approach to authority.

Where Do You Stand?

It is at this moment in our trainings that we pause and ask participants to do out loud what many of them may have been doing for the past several minutes. That is, we ask them to think and reflect on where they find themselves in this framework. I'd like you to take a moment now to do the same thing. To help in this process, here are some guiding questions:

- Where do you find yourself in the social discipline window most of the time? You have to choose just one box.
- Was that challenging? Did you find yourself between two boxes, three boxes, or all four?
- What influences the box you might find yourself within?
- Are you in a different box at work than at home? With your colleagues as opposed to clients? If so, why is that, and how is that working for you?

This always sparks the greatest conversation and deepest analysis around Restorative Practices. We will continue to reference the Social Discipline Window throughout the book, as it is truly the basis for all of this work. Additionally, we explore it within our work and life contexts in upcoming chapters, as well as handle questions that it may raise in Chapter Eight.

The Least You Should Know

- Understanding how we use our authority is one of the most restorative insights we can have.
- It considers how our tendencies to (1) challenge and (2) connect with others can combine to create the four ways most of us use our authority:
    o We choose to abdicate our authority and NOT act as leaders, NOT engage. (Low challenge, low connection.)
    o We do things TO people in an authoritarian way. (High challenge, low connection.)
    o We abandon accountability and do things FOR people, causing dependency and stifling people's own agency. (Low challenge, high connection.)
    o We collaborate WITH the people we serve, both holding them accountable and respecting their needs and ideas. (High challenge, high connection.)
- Restorative Practices require us to operate from the WITH mindset. This does not come naturally to most of us.
- Both personal and systemic factors influence which of the four approaches is our default.

5   Shame that Hurts, Shame that Helps

"Shame in the social emotional world is analogous to pain in the physical world. I don't want to live in it, but life without it would be equally horrible." —Steve Korr

Honestly, I never gave any thought to shame prior to my introduction to Restorative Practices. I probably considered shame as negative in a general sense but didn't reflect on what it meant in statements like "shame on you" or "you should be ashamed of yourself." I admit that I've used both of these frequently while wagging my finger at my children or dogs. I'm sure that what I was trying to convey is that the recipient (especially the dogs) should feel "bad" about what they did. What I wanted was a deep feeling of conviction and remorse for doing something that I didn't like. Of course, I linked it to some rule that was broken, but really, I was talking about the harm the behavior caused me and others.

What does shame have to do with the restoration process? How can shame be destructive to both ourselves and others? How can shame be harnessed to help transform behavior and bring people into good standing with those they have harmed?

Nathan Harris and Shadd Maruna address these questions in their 2005 article "Shame, Shaming and Restorative Justice: A Critical Appraisal":

"The concept of shame is indeed a dangerous emotion, but rather than trying to avoid it (which is probably impossible), restorative justice interventions are well suited to the task of managing and working constructively with the shame that all parties experience in situations of crime and conflict."

Shame is a cornerstone concept in Restorative Practices. An in-depth analysis of shame is beyond the scope of this book. Instead, I will provide a brief introduction to how I think of shame as it relates to Restorative Practices. Personally, I lean heavily on John Braithwaite's reintegrative shaming theory (RST) in my understanding of shame and shaming. In this chapter we will use RST as a foundation to tackle the shame that hurts and the shame that helps..

Defining Shame

In a general sense, according to psychologist Janice Lindsay-Hartz, shame can be understood as a concern about others' disapproval, a negative evaluation of the self, and feelings of having done wrong. Harris and Maruna further explain that "the word 'shame' derives from Old Germanic roots meaning to clothe or cover oneself, and in Greek the same word (pudenda) is used to refer to both shame and human genitalia. Shame, then, refers to an experience of exposure—as in the proverb 'shame dwells in the eyes'."

> ## Shame and the Nine Affects
>
> In my restorative practice, I've decided to focus less on the role of affect psychology, especially as it relates to shame. I've found less of a connection to its definition of shame as an "interruption of positive affect" than to the work of Braithwaite's reintegrative shaming theory. However, the work of Silvan Tomkins and Donald Nathanson are important to the field of restorative practices. Their work on the nine affects are referenced regularly by colleagues I respect and admire.

Shame also exists because of our collective adherence to the "just world theory." We all know the theory well, as it is the basis of our upbringing and most institutions. It essentially goes like this:

- Good things happen to good people.
- Bad things happen to bad people.
- Therefore, if something bad happens, it is because I deserve it because I'm bad, or
- I'm a good person so what happened to me wasn't really "bad."

As you can imagine, this type of thinking can skew one's understanding of blame and responsibility for heinous acts like rape, domestic violence, slavery, etc. It can lead us toward self-deprecation on the one hand, or denial on the other. It can also live inside those of us with authority, leading us to believe that there are no real unjust practices, only people getting what they deserve, and that our own rise to a position of authority validates our goodness and the rightness of whatever decisions we make.

Shame appears when 1) the "good" person realizes or perceives that they have done a bad thing, or 2) when a bad thing happens to a "good" person. The cognitive reconciliation necessary here with the just world theory often produces shame. In other words, people who've previously thought of themselves as "good" are suddenly faced with the possibility that they are "bad."

But all shame isn't made equal. Let's explore Braithwaite's concepts of stigmatizing shame versus reintegrative shame. Some experts have labeled all shame as problematic and hurtful. According to Harris and Maruna, author and psychiatrist James Gilligan "explicitly equates shaming with 'mocking,' 'despising' and 'scorning' and uses the term 'shame' to refer to a deep-rooted sense of personal worthlessness." I understand his criticism of shame given that definition. For instance, we can imagine the harm that scores of women faced by stepping forward to share their stories of sexual assault prior to the #MeToo movement. The movement was launched to challenge the stigmatizing shame that women were facing both personally and publicly.

What is being described here is stigmatizing shame, which is always corrosive and nonrestorative. It includes several significant characteristics:

- It embeds wrongdoing inside of the person, creating a sense of personal failure.
- It is not terminated by forgiveness, meaning that there is no process for returning to "good standing."
- It relies on immutable negative labels such as "criminal," "violator," and "evil."
- It is disintegrative, in that it disconnects the person being shamed from their community, family, or team.
- It results in greater levels of wrongdoing (e.g. "I'll continue to

do 'bad' because I am 'bad'").

This is what I've noticed that school represents for too many students. If school is a site of negative shaming and stigmatization through labeling certain students as problems, the institution helps to further alienate them from the very social embeddedness that would help improve their school behavior and performance. We can hear a painful logic in the following statement I received from a former student:

"Look, Dr. Muhammad, my school doesn't like me and I don't like it. If they are going to mess with me every time I go there by suspending me because of the way that I dress or for other dumb stuff, then I'm not gonna go or I'm going to go and act up so that I don't have to be there. They don't care about me, man. They tell me that I need that paper [diploma] but I gotta find another way."

For this young man, school was a place where he experienced shame and disconnection. In exchange, his teachers and administrators also likely felt shame at their inability to help the student succeed. Does the student have responsibility here for his misbehavior and success? Absolutely! Does the school have responsibility here for its level of connection (or lack thereof) and his success? Absolutely! However, when the shame that exists within the student and the shame that exists within the school staff are unreconciled, they stigmatize each other. For the student, the school is to blame because it doesn't care. For the school, the student is to blame for acting out and causing problems. Both the student and the school deflect responsibility onto the other, transforming their shame into blame.

According to Harris and Maruna, "shame is most problematic when it is unacknowledged, unresolved, and hence becomes projected on to others in a scapegoat fashion." This is stigmatizing shame, the shame that hurts.

Reintegrative Shame: The Shame That Helps

A certain level of physical pain is necessary for our survival. When we put our hand too close to a fire and our skin starts to burn, we know to pull our hand back. When we get a bad sore throat, we know to visit the doctor and get medicine for strep throat. Pain helps us understand the limits of our physical behavior and, when necessary, get the medical treatment we need to heal.

It is the same with shame; it can help us to survive within a society and understand the limits and impact of our social behavior. When shame is handled within a supportive, yet challenging process, it can lead to restoration. This is called reintegrative shame.

When we operate in the WITH box, we are naturally led toward a reintegrative approach to shame. We let our subordinate know how their poor behavior negatively impacted the team, but we give them a chance to make it up on the next project. We tell a child how upsetting it is for them to leave the room messy, but then we hug the child and reaffirm that they are a wonderful part of the family. We ask our younger sister to discuss her feelings about her current mediocre grades and help her develop a plan of action for success next semester. These are examples of reintegrative shame in action. We are communicating that they are not in "right" standing now AND that they are still connected to this community. As such, they have a responsibility to do something to make things better.

Two important pieces of the reintegrative shame process are 1) the separation of the deed and the doer, and 2) the focus on the harm instead of the rule broken.

When we separate the deed from the doer, we are doing what the fourth century African bishop Saint Augustine admonished us to do: "love the sinner, but hate the sin." He understood that the most effective way to help transform a failing monk to have the strength to move beyond his vice and return to the righteous path was through connection (love the sinner) and challenge (hate the sin).

The practices explained in Part Two will allow participants in a conflict to share their stories and express the impact of the harm. This engages all parties in the difficult work of helping people who have caused harm, people who have been harmed, and their supporters acknowledge, work through, and ultimately resolve any shame they may be experiencing.

Reintegrative shame necessarily involves the acknowledgment of wrongdoing and is linked with building empathy for those hurt. However, stigmatizing shame is an unresolved shame that results in an inability to settle issues and deepens feelings of hostility towards others.

The Compass of Shame

We all face shame regularly. Avoiding shame altogether is probably an impossibility, and it should be. How it is processed by the collective, through reintegration or stigmatization, is critical to a positive outcome. How it is managed on the individual level is equally as important. Donald Nathanson, in *Shame and Pride: Affect, Sex, and the Birth of the Self*, identified four ways that we avoid dealing effectively with an experience of shame. He called this the Compass of Shame.

The Compass describes a common set of responses to an experience of shame. Each exists on a range from subtle responses (towards the center of the compass) to more extreme behaviors (towards the poles). All are problematic because they stand in the way of examining and addressing what the shame is highlighting about us and our behavior. Let's tackle each one.

Attack Others

When facing shame, sometimes we "go for the jugular" by hitting below the belt at someone's sensitive issues. We shift the blame or try to make someone else smaller. We might relish telling people the negative things we think about them. It might range from banter (mocking and joking) at another's expense to threats and violence. When we are expressing shame by attacking others, we lessen the pain of shame by making someone else the target. We seek shelter by invalidating others.

Avoidance

Sometimes we lessen the pain of shame by diverting attention away from the experience and onto some part of ourselves that is not "defective." We might use humor to hide or distract from emotional pain. We restore some element of individual status by drawing the focus to something in ourselves that is a source of pride. We might use our enhanced body image, achievements, or possessions as a show-piece, only showing others one part of ourselves. We might overindulge in drugs or alcohol to stay unaware of our feelings. We avoid the pain of shame by hiding from ourselves.

Attack Self

We sometimes attempt to lessen the shame by regaining control of the situation through self-condemnation. Maybe it's self-deprecating humor or more self-destructive behaviors like cutting and self-harm. This sometimes looks like when we put ourselves down in conversations so that others won't take the chance to do it first. When we only see ourselves through the lens of victimhood or don't recognize our own sense of agency, we are also attacking ourselves. In all these responses, we ineffectively respond to shame by invalidating ourselves.

Compass of Shame

Withdrawal

Attack Others

Attack Self

Avoidance

Withdrawal

When we "run" and disconnect from others to avoid presumed judgement, we are often attempting to manage the pain of shame. This might look like isolating ourselves in front of a TV instead of visiting friends when we are troubled. While it is culturally dependent, the downcast face of someone experiencing shame is a typical withdrawal response. I've found it hard for myself and others to maintain eye contact with someone while experiencing shame. We try to alleviate the negative effect of shame by "removing" ourselves from the glare of others. We physically or emotionally withdraw in order to hide from our shame.

Using the Compass as a Tool

I've found that many of us have a default response to shame on the Compass. Mine is to attack others. Through some hard self-reflection and with the help of being married to a clinical psychologist, I've realized (and been told directly by her) that I step in and towards others, teeth bared and fists ready, when I'm negatively processing shame. This makes sense and probably aligns logically with my own struggle in the TO box. I'm still on the journey with this!

When presenting the Compass of Shame to people, they find their own connection to it like they do with the Social Discipline Window. An interesting difference is that the Compass is also a powerful tool to help us humanize others, particularly those we are in conflict with. When a staff member is irate and abusive because they missed a quarterly bonus by five points on their evaluation, could it be a shame response that leads them to attack others?

A child puts their hoodie up to cover their face while a parent is lecturing to them about their chores. Could this be withdrawal? Might a family member who obsesses over working out, spending three hours in the gym every day, be practicing avoidance? Does the overweight colleague who always jokes about his weight try to lessen the shame by attacking himself?

By using the Compass in this way, it encourages us to stay curious about the observed behavior and might help humanize other people for us. They are not necessarily just a jerk, ignoring us, distracting, or self-absorbed. They might be a human having a negative response to shame. We might understand that because we sometimes have similar responses, too.

Managing Shame

If shame can hurt and help, how do we manage it effectively? On the individual level, we have a responsibility to our emotional health to

1) recognize what our default shame response might be.
2) be open to understanding what the feeling of shame is trying to tell us about an experience.
3) acknowledge that we are not the problem, but that the problem is the problem.
4) when things get overwhelming, reach out for support to our tribe (family, colleagues, or friends) or a mental health professional.

A wonderful resource for this individual work is Dr. Christina Watlington, whom I have referenced throughout this book. She can be found at www.drwatlington.com. Another resource is the *Real Solution Anger Management Workbook* by Richard H. Pfeiffer. In it, he offers several techniques, including "Shame-Busting Statements." A few include "I release and forgive everyone who didn't support my changes," "I control my responses to stressful situations," and "I am open and honest about my feelings and express them well."

On the collective level, managing shame is essentially what all the tools of Restorative Practices help accomplish. We identify when it shows up by using the Compass of Shame. We realize when we initiate it ourselves through the Punitive Model and TO, FOR, and NOT approaches in the Social Discipline Window. In Part Two, we will explore the restorative practices that will help to move people out of stigmatizing shame, away from the negative responses on the Compass of Shame, and into restoration using reintegrative shame through connection and challenge.

Travel Notes from the Journey

By 2017, the time had come in my professional life when I had to leap. I had a side hustle training and speaking through the company I'd founded, Akoben, and I had reached a point where if I didn't start giving it more cultivation and attention, I would need to let it go and stay focused on my day job running multiple state human services operations. By this point in my Restorative Journey, I had a set of people in my tribe whom I was deeply connected to and who were empowered to challenge me regularly. Honestly, sometimes I felt hammered and avoided their texts. I missed our scheduled check-in calls. On the Compass of Shame I was practicing classic withdrawal. My fear of success and self-doubt about possibly being a fraud (who was I but a grown-up version of a poor kid anyway?) was in overdrive. I felt shame around wanting wild success, so much more than my parents had achieved, and shame for doubting myself as well. When they conspired and tracked me down, my good friend Govindh Jayaraman asked me a powerfully reintegrative question: "Malik, how does playing small impact your family?" He made me remember that I was a part of a collective, my family, that needed and wanted me to pull my shoulders back, raise my eyes to the horizon, and leap. I've realized that I can and do most often reconcile shame by leaning towards, not away from, the community.

The Least You Should Know

- Shame arises when we sense others' disapproval, evaluate ourselves negatively, or feel that we've done something wrong.
- Shame can be either stigmatizing (hurtful) or reintegrative (helpful).
  - Stigmatizing shame is shame we either don't deserve or haven't processed appropriately. It causes us to feel we are permanently flawed, disconnect from our community, and commit additional wrongs.
  - Reintegrative shame helps us see where we went wrong, repair that wrong, and make changes so we are less likely to commit further wrong acts. It accomplishes all this while letting us know we are valued and supported.
- The Compass of Shame describes four ways we often avoid dealing with shame effectively: through attacking others, avoidance, attacking ourselves, and withdrawal.

Part Two: Practices

"Neo, sooner or later you're going to realize just as I did that there's a difference between knowing the path and walking the path."
—Laurence Fishburne as Morpheus in The Matrix

"Thought without action is blind." —Kwame Nkrumah

6 Wielding Affective Language

"Staying vulnerable is a risk we have to take if we want to experience connection." –Dr. Brené Brown

"It is better to whisper in their language than to yell in our own." –Govindh Jayaraman

It continues to fascinate me that all the organizations we've worked with have had one thing in common, whether they were big or small, private or public, for profit or not for profit, in the field of business or of education: they cite communication as their greatest challenge. In fact, we notice the same trend when working with parents, couples, and families; in faith-based organizations; and on sports teams. Communication—the kind, quality, and lack thereof—ranks among our most challenging core issues as human beings.

What contribution does Restorative Practices make towards addressing our fundamental issues of communication? When we are working to restore and repair relationships, as I discussed in Chapter Three, community and connection are critical first steps. When we're developing those connections, there is one element of communication that is essential for us to hear and understand each other: affective language. However, before we delve into what affective language is and why it is important, let's explore how we communicate in general.

Using our Emotional vs. Behavioral vocabulary

Dr. Christina Watlington, a clinical psychologist, often states that "in the absence of a strong emotional vocabulary, we all rely on our behavioral vocabulary." What does this mean? In the absence of access to language which expresses affect, emotion, and feelings (i.e. our emotional vocabulary), we will communicate what is going on with us through our behavior. Here are some examples:

- If the student doesn't feel safe or skilled enough to raise her hand and express frustration and confusion, she may express her insecurity through her nonverbal behavior, ranging from a dazed look of mental detachment to an aggressive backlash against the teacher or other students.

- If the staff member doesn't have the words to express his burnout and feelings of being overwhelmed, he might avoid work or disrespect his colleagues.

- If the leader doesn't feel comfortable sharing her concerns and frustrations with her direct reports, then she may express this through giving them the cold shoulder or firing someone without due process.

If we can understand that this is a universal phenomenon affecting us all, it might allow us to have more patience and recognize the humanity of folks when they struggle. For instance, I'm an emotional eater. It's taken me a few decades and the benefit of having a psychologist as a spouse to come to this conclusion. What this means for me is that when I'm stressed, upset, happy, frustrated, excited, angry, tired, or ashamed, I eat. And eat. And eat. Mostly carbs and non-nutritional food in the form of waffle fries, buffalo wings, sweet tea, etc. I've come to realize, after some hard work and health scares, that eating is my default behavioral vocabulary to ineffectively communicate my emotions. For some people, like me, that default behavior is food. For others, it could be avoiding, yelling, hitting, drinking, working out excessively, invading personal space, etc.

Now, what happens when someone doesn't just struggle to verbally express emotion, but when it is socially unacceptable and, in some cases, dangerous to do so? What happens when the pressure to deny all but a few emotions is intimately wrapped up in the core of your self-identity? What happens when anger, pride, and happiness are the full range of your emotional continuum, and they become the filter through which you manifest shame, humiliation, sadness, and fear?

Many people in our society struggle with these challenges. And this is especially true for boys and men, and even more so with our boys and men of color, who represent, in the Western psyche, the quintessential male other. They are born into a patriarchal society whose norms expect men to be strong and powerful. However, due to their race, boys and men of color are economically and socially marginalized and therefore do not have access to the White male power and economic structure. In the quest to achieve a semblance of masculine power, in a society which prioritizes it above all else, boys of color are often more likely to manifest forms of masculinity detrimental to their health and often to their communities, as well. The culture of masculinity and hypermasculinity asks men to be strong at all times, and therefore it prevents them (us) from expressing what George M. Taylor refers to as "our inner lives and truths." I discuss this in more detail in our workshops and in the forthcoming book *We Can Save Our Boys of Color.*

But no matter our gender or race, even the most emotionally intelligent people among us can struggle to communicate effectively.

Learning about affective language can help us all become more effective communicators. This is especially vital within a restorative culture.

What is Affective Language?

We refer to the ability to express the full range of emotion verbally as "wielding affective language." That is, it is the ability to communicate verbally when we are sad, frustrated, overjoyed, ashamed, and fascinated. It requires us not just to have a wide vocabulary at our disposal, but also to have the ability to connect this emotional vocabulary to our own internal experience of feelings and emotions.

Just like the development and understanding of any language, affective language is taught, encouraged, and refined. We teach affective language through both modeling and explicit instruction. When we make Affective Statements or ask Restorative Questions, we are engaging in the process of modeling and teaching affective language. Let's explore both Affective Statements and Restorative Questions as basic skills in your Restorative toolbox.

Affective Statements

Affective Statements are often simple, yet profoundly powerful statements we make to let the recipient know how their behavior impacted us.

Affective Statements:
"I" statements that express emotion and are connected to behavior

Here are some examples of Affective Statements:

- "Malik, I am excited because you came to the center today prepared with your tutoring materials and a positive attitude."
- "Lisa, when you were cursing in front of the elderly women on the field trip, I felt (and still feel) embarrassed and frustrated."
- "I'm confused and angry right now, Javier, because you promised us that you would be here at noon, but you're late again."

In our trainings, I anchor the use of Affective Statements with a personal story from my time as a principal of an alternative school. As mentioned earlier, my default leadership style is the TO approach, and early in my career I was known for being very much of a TO kind of leader, among both the students and staff. However, at the time, I was deepening my understanding and connection to Restorative Practices and was eager to practice the material in real time. One day, as I entered the middle school wing, I noticed a teacher in the distance standing alone outside of his classroom. When he saw me, he quickly turned and headed inside. Considering we were in the middle of a class period, I couldn't understand why he would leave his classroom unsupervised. I was halfway down the corridor when I heard a familiar student's voice yell, "I don't give a fuck about Mr. Muhammad!" It was coming from the same classroom. Within a few seconds, I was at the doorway, filling it with my oversized frame and dominant personality. I was able to quickly scan the room and gauge the scene. A student named Travis had essentially taken over the classroom, entertaining everyone with his best Kevin Hart impression. Although this was English class, Travis, reinforced by his audience of peers, had taken over the show and threatened the teacher when he tried to intervene. Mr. Graves, the teacher, had stepped into the hallway to take a few mindful breaths and get centered before returning to challenge Travis. Apparently, upon returning and warning the student that he would call Mr. Muhammad (the TO dominant principal), Travis made it very clear that he was not alarmed through his profane exclamation.

Travis had yet to see me when I first entered the classroom, and I could tell he didn't understand why people had stopped laughing at his impersonation. However, when one of his peers made my presence known, Travis did an amazingly agile 180° spin while taking his seat and putting on his best innocent look. If I hadn't been so frustrated, I would have been impressed. That frustration showed up as anger on my face, and the other students tried to move their desks away from Travis's.

I asked Travis to come into the hallway with me, and although at first he refused, he eventually slow-walked himself to the gallows. During those long seconds, I was making a decision. Was I going to default into my comfort zone and drop the figurative hammer on him, or was I going to practice this Restorative stuff when it was still new and hard to do? Was there anything I could do right now that would allow me to effectively communicate to Travis, while maintaining our connection and my sense of authority?

I had an idea just as he shuffled into the hallway. Before I could say anything, he launched into his version of an apology, which sounded like, "Ah, Mr. Muhammad, my bad, my bad. I didn't mean to curse in your school my bad." He stopped short when he looked up at my face. I was doing my best to express the emotions I was feeling at the time: sadness and disappointment. He had expected anger, so he was visibly confused. I told him I was disappointed that he was disturbing his entire English class and cheating himself and his peers out of the lesson. I let that sit with him for a moment. I imagine that had some impact, but disappointment from adults was a normal experience for him. I then told him what I really needed to say, how I really felt: "Travis, I'm sad that you said that you don't give a fuck about Mr. Muhammad. I'm sad because we know each other, I care about you, and I would never say that about you, Travis." His immediate response was powerful. This hardened, amazing young man looked astonished and confused. Here I was, this alpha male, this larger-than-life school leader, defying the norms of hypermasculinity and telling a thirteen-year-old boy that I was hurt by his behavior. He didn't know what to say. My spirit moved me to continue. Rather than send him home or take some other punitive action, I told him that he had to report now to the Reflection Room to process his violation of our norm about profanity and classroom disruption. I also told him that by the end of the day, he, Mr. Graves, and I were going to come back together to understand what had happened and what needed to happen to make things right. He left with his head down to the Reflection Room. He eventually returned to his classes. It was reported to me that the normally verbose and gregarious Travis was unusually quiet throughout the rest of the day. He participated in class but was more reserved. His teachers were thankful.

I pulled Travis and Mr. Graves together a few minutes before dismissal and we processed what had happened using the Restorative Questions (covered later in this chapter). I learned that he had just seen the new Kevin Hart movie before anyone else and was excited to spoil the best parts, and that he was embarrassed and upset when Mr. Graves "interrupted" him by telling him I was coming down the hallway. Mr. Graves expressed to Travis how his behavior led to his own shame in not being able to control the classroom and embarrassment in front of his boss. We then talked about how to make this right. It took a few minutes for us to work out a process for Travis to shine in the class (to get his needs met), without disrupting the classroom (to meet the needs of others). This was great, but the real magic happened at the end of the conversation. Travis, that beautiful and challenging young man in an alternative school, said the most beautiful thing that a student has ever said to me. He looked me in the eye, and with all of the sincerity he could muster, he said, "Mr. Muhammad, I want you to know that I really do give a fuck about you!" I believe that I had to wipe the tears from my eyes as I gave that young man a hug.

What Travis had expected was punishment, but what he got was connection. What he was prepared for was to be yelled at and reprimanded for breaking rules and disturbing class. While profanity in school is not okay, and stealing time away from instruction is not okay, what Travis was really doing was breaking our social contract, first by putting his need for attention above others' needs (his peers' and Mr. Graves'), and then by violating our relationship by making that statement about me. The Affective Statement I used allowed him to understand that his behavior had negatively impacted others. A mere trip to the Reflection Room, a detention, or a suspension would not have accomplished this.

Why Don't We Do This More Often?

In our trainings, after defining Affective Statements for participants, we ask them if they make these types of statements on a regular basis. After a brief pause, many people raise their hands to indicate that they do. They say that they feel rather comfortable with expressing emotions with those whom they work with and serve. We then do a quick exercise that goes something like this:

Facilitator: "Okay, let's talk about what happens when someone we work with does something wrong. Let's think about the things we say when they mess up, break a rule, or violate a norm. Let's call out the statements that we make."

After a few minutes we've created a good list of the statements. Regardless of whether the participants are speaking to adults in a company, kids in a school, or even their own children, the statements are inevitably variations of these:

"What were you thinking?" "Are you serious?"
"That's not cool!" "Well, you've got a warning"
"C'mon Man!" "Really?"
"I'm not even trying to hear that!" "Is this how you treat your family?"
"You are not living up to your "I'm tired of this!"
potential."

None of these responses is necessarily negative on its own, and all may be valid. However, what they all have in common is that they are not Affective Statements. When we process the activity with the participants, almost none of the statements they ever call out are Affective Statements, despite having just discussed and defined them for the group. This real-time data shows how rarely we communicate to others how their behavior actually affects us.

Regardless of the type of organization, from education to business, and across all demographics, our experience is that the overwhelming majority of what we say when confronting negative behavior is not an Affective Statement. When we process this with workshop participants, I ask a simple question: Why don't we make Affective Statements when confronted with negative behavior? There are three common responses:

- These statements take time.
- I wasn't familiar with this concept.
- I'm afraid to be vulnerable.

Lack of Time

Usually, the first objection to Affective Statements is both an affirmation of how important they can be followed by an explanation that we don't make these statements because they take time. I usually grin in response to this one, and the person who offered it frowns because they know they are about to be challenged. I ask someone with a stopwatch to determine how long it takes for the person to recite the following two statements. The results are below:

Statement	Average Time
"What's wrong with you?"	1.58 seconds
"I feel disrespected when you interrupt me while speaking."	3.10 seconds

In terms of time, the difference is a mere 1.52 seconds. 1.52 seconds! This is equivalent to two blinks of your eye. Yet, in terms of impact, the difference is significant. The first statement is most often received as accusatory and promotes defensiveness. And, if we are being honest, we don't really want to know what is "wrong with them." We already have our own ideas about what they are up to, what the hell they are thinking, and what mental disorder we believe they might have. On the other hand, the second statement allows us the emotional release of telling them what is going on with us in response to them. It communicates clearly that we are not okay with what they did. We gain this, all for the small sacrifice of a mere 1.52 seconds!

When unpacking the time excuse further, we learn that making Affective Statements leads into an actual conversation with the person, which will, in fact, take more time. In other words, by letting the person know how their behavior impacted us, we now probably have to talk to them more about it. Too often, we don't want that level of engagement and would prefer to make our statement at them and keep it moving.

However, having a long conversation that has the potential to change a person's behavior saves time in the long run. We've all experienced the cycle of *negative behavior* ➤ *correction* ➤ *negative behavior* ➤ *correction* that the Punitive Model perpetuates. Arguably, the time that is spent processing Affective Statements can interrupt this cycle. The next-level conversation that Affective Statements promote is actually the most essential part of the behavior's consequence. This conversation is what helps change the behavior in the future.

Lack of Familiarity

The second most common explanation for not offering Affective Statements regularly is due to a lack of familiarity with making them. The idea here is that of course we don't tell people how their behavior impacts us because we don't normally do that; we don't have practice or comfort with expressing ourselves in this way. On face value, this seems like a reasonable statement. After all, who can fault us for not doing something that we never knew how to do anyway? However, the fundamental problem with this rationale is that most of us do make Affective Statements regularly. In positive contexts, most of us are very comfortable with letting people know how their behavior impacts us. For instance, these are commonly heard Affective Statements:

- I'm really excited that you came to the meeting today.
- When I heard that you crushed that test, I was so proud.
- I'm really happy that you worked out that issue with Jamal.
- When you kissed me for the first time, my heart was overjoyed!

These expressions meet all of the criteria for an Affective Statement, and we are probably comfortable making them. We didn't have formal training on this, and most of us didn't need coaching because it is culturally normal for us to let the people around us know when we feel positively about what they do. We intuitively know that these expressions draw us closer by strengthening our connection. We want them to know how we feel, and in fact, sometimes we feel obligated to let them know how we feel. However, why is it not natural for most of us to also let people know when we feel negatively about their behavior as well? I believe the next section explains this best.

Fear of Vulnerability

In our workshops, after some prodding while processing this activity, someone eventually raises the biggest barrier we have with Affective Statements: They require us to be vulnerable. Most of us are not comfortable with that. Heads nod, and we begin to unpack the concept of vulnerability. As it turns out, many of us are not okay with directly telling someone who frustrated/upset/disappointed/annoyed/angered us that they did so and how they did it. Some of us are very comfortable with yelling at or negatively shaming them. Others are talented at being sarcastic or passive-aggressive with the person. Most of us are gifted at talking about them to others.

This impulse to respond to harm with negative statements is connected to our unconscious bent toward the Punitive Model. The Punitive Model, as it's expressed in our criminal justice system, teaches us that when someone hurts us, the justice we deserve is seeing them suffer in return, by losing privileges, going to prison, or even losing their life. Similarly, our instinctive response to people who've wronged us is usually to throw something back at them that subtly (or not so subtly) insults them. This eye-for-an-eye response to conflict might feel satisfying in the moment, but it serves only to further disconnect us at best, and at worst actually escalates the situation, leading to further conflict and harm. It also causes us to distance ourselves from our truer, deeper feelings about what has happened, which include shame.

If we can get comfortable with Affective Statements, we can begin to change the language we use to respond to harm. But this doesn't come naturally for most of us. Even though almost all of us are comfortable making Affective Statements to express positive emotion, few people seem able to apply this same level of comfort to

Affective Statements about negative emotions. We agree that this primarily comes from a fear of vulnerability.

There is a natural hesitation to expose your feelings to the very person who just caused harm. These are some of the internal questions we are faced with in these moments:

- What if they get a rise out of seeing how they impacted me?
- What if they take my disclosure for weakness?
- Am I not being a good professional/adult/leader/parent if I show how they "got" to me?
- Am I taking this too personally?
- What if they respond by saying that they don't care how it impacted me?
- Are you asking me to cut myself and bleed in front of the shark?

The fear of being vulnerable is the primary cause for why we struggle to make Affective Statements which express "negative" impact. However, it's precisely by being vulnerable that we humanize ourselves, even to those who have caused harm. It is by being vulnerable that we allow them to see that we are, in fact, inside of a bi-directional relationship where their behavior affects us and ours affects them. It is through the Affective Statement that we show them the impact of their behavior, and it is by making that same Affective Statement that we hope to impact theirs.

In her fantastic TED talk "The Power of Vulnerability," Dr. Brené Brown asserts that vulnerability is at the "core of shame, fear, disconnection and worthiness" as well as the "birthplace of joy, love, creativity and belonging." Becoming vulnerable through making Affective Statements situates us perfectly in a place of uncertainty. How will they respond? Is this emotionally safe? What if they say that they don't care how their behavior impacted me?

To be honest, I don't know if any of us ever gets completely comfortable with being vulnerable, whether within the context of making Affective Statements or otherwise. Vulnerability is always scary. I still get butterflies sometimes when I sit down with someone to have one of these conversations. However, there is a simple but powerful reason for us to make the statements regardless: They help us connect by being seen as a human being.

When we express affect through statements linking other people's behavior to our emotions, we underscore the fact that we are in a relationship, whether personal or professional, where actions and feelings matter. We highlight the reality that we are a human being worthy of acknowledgment, and they are a human being worthy of engagement. In a very real sense, the Affective Statement is the embodiment of the Connection/Challenge paradigm. Through the Affective Statement, we communicate our connection because we are saying, "I see you, and now you see me. We are in a dynamic bi-directional relationship." We are also saying, "I love/respect/value you enough to tell you how you impacted me."

Restorative Questions

> **"The antidote to assumptions is curiosity."**
> —Dr. Christina Watlington

The power of this quote by Dr. Watlington is that it anchors our ability to ask questions against the problematic nature of assumptions. Of course, assumptions are the genesis of bias and prejudice. However, we can combat this when we choose, instead, to ask questions. The set of Restorative Questions that we will describe here is a tool to use with those who have caused harm and and/or been harmed. They were originally developed by Terry O'Connell in his work conducting restorative conferences in Australia. I've modified them slightly to reflect our experiences in asking them to youth and adults in conflict.

Ultimately, these questions allow us to unpack thoughts, emotions, accountability, and needs. They also help us develop an action plan for restoration. That's a tall order for just five questions!

In *Community: The Structure of Belonging,* Peter Block argues why we should have a bias towards powerful questions instead of our typical tendency to give advice or ask weak, superficial questions of those we serve:

"Questions create the space for something new to emerge. [When we only give advice or ask superficial questions] the hidden agenda is to maintain dominance and to be right. A great question has three qualities: it is ambiguous, personal, and evokes anxiety."

Now, I believe that when Peter talks about evoking anxiety, he means it in the sense of causing psychological pause to really reflect on the question. A good Restorative Question should be weighty enough to be worthy of causing pause before responding. In the work of addressing, processing, and repairing harm, here are the powerful Restorative Questions we can use:

The Narrative Question
What Happened?

The Antecedent Question
What Were You Thinking at the Time?

The Remorse Question
What Have You Been Thinking About Since ?

The Shame Question
Who Has Been Affected/ Impacted and How?

The Repair Question
What Needs To Happen To Make Things Right/Better?

Let's break down the logic and impact of each question.

What happened?

The power of this question lives within its simplicity. It's a non-judgmental launch into what is often a powerful conversation. Rather than asking "What did you do?" or using a similar construction that implies blame, this question offers the respondent an opportunity to share their experience in the incident. It shows that we are approaching the conversation with an open mind and helping them to be in a place of engagement early on.

What were you thinking at the time?

This is called the antecedent, or function, question. For someone who has caused harm, this question allows them to express their reasoning and explain their mindset at the time of the wrongdoing. We can discover their triggers and interpretations of others' behaviors and learn how they might have mislabeled or misrecognized the situation. This question further communicates that they are seen as a full human, with thoughts and ideas worth hearing.

What have you been thinking about since?

Sometimes, we immediately regret the harm that we've caused. At other times, it takes distance to properly process what happened and our role in the incident. And sometimes, we don't get there until challenged by others in a process like this one. This third question provides the opportunity to directly address their mindset "postmortem." This question also helps us gauge where the respondent is on the remorse continuum:

My colleagues and I developed this continuum in order to help explain what we have observed during this process. Of course, this continuum mirrors the stages of grief intentionally. It also begins to perhaps unpack a background of shame present in both the wrongdoer and the person who was harmed. By asking "what have you been thinking about since?" we are able to further their process of self-reflection.

Additionally, in the Punitive Paradigm mentioned in Chapter Two, the person who's caused harm naturally begins to see him/herself as the victim. An employee might sit at home during an administrative suspension, a student might sit outside of the principal's office after a behavioral referral, or a young man might pace in a holding cell after an assault. Often, they are brooding over what happened to them, how they might be or have been mistreated. How unfair the process is against them. This is not to downplay the reality of oppression and prejudice, but what we often don't see within this model is the shift in focus to the harm they have caused. This question gives us and them the opportunity to begin to understand what they have been fretting about, if anything. And we hit the idea of causing harm even more squarely in the next question.

Who was impacted and how?

This is the powerful reintegrative shame question. This allows us to really explore and develop an understanding of the ripple effect of harmful actions. We have established or reaffirmed connection and the humanity of the wrongdoer with the first three questions, and now we push them to confront how they have impacted others. It is through asking this question—sometimes gently, sometimes firmly, but almost always repeatedly—that the fog of denial and downplaying clears and the person begins to feel the full weight of their actions. They confront the fact that it wasn't just the teacher impacted by their outburst, but the other students, the principal, their parents, and the classroom next door as well. They come to realize that by stealing that car they not only hurt the owner, but his children who now missed three days of school. This question helps the person who is chronically late to work acknowledge that all members of their team must work harder because of them, and that they harm their supervisor, who feels compelled to make excuses for their behavior. By asking this question, and staying on it for a little while, we provide the responder with the opportunity to see and carry the full weight of their

~Travel Tip~

The question "Who was impacted and how?" is so important that you should stay on that question for some time. Repeatedly ask the person the question to explore who else might have been impacted and how. You want them to "feel" the full weight of their actions.

actions that is theirs to own and carry. Essentially, we allow them to confront their shame and experience it reintegratively.

What needs to happen in order to make things right/better?

If we have done a good job with the last question, then the impact of their actions is weighing heavily on the shoulders of the wrongdoer. To end the process there would probably lead to stigmatizing shame and be counterproductive at best, punitive at worst. What makes this process restorative is this last question, squarely focused on repair and accountability. When we ask the wrongdoer "What needs to happen in order to make things right or better?" we are doing at least two things:

First, we are challenging them to step up, own the impact of their behavior, think about needs, and execute on a path to restore and repair.

Second, we are instilling hope. They have just had to sit with and face the ripple effect of harm in the previous question, and now they get to understand that they have the opportunity to alleviate some of that shame by working towards healing and restoration. They have the responsibility—and might have the privilege—of making it right and working towards being in "right standing" once again.

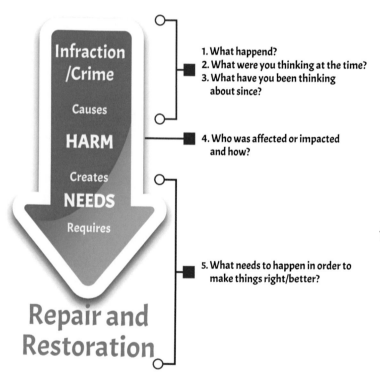

Infraction /Crime

Causes

HARM

Creates

NEEDS

Requires

Repair and Restoration

1. What happend?
2. What were you thinking at the time?
3. What have you been thinking about since?

4. Who was affected or impacted and how?

5. What needs to happen in order to make things right/better?

In basic terms, the first three questions are anchored in the spirit of connection and support. The last two are anchored in challenge and accountability. The whole process itself is restorative.

Notice that we deliberately avoid two things. First, we don't ask "Why?". This most frequently asked question often leads to defensiveness and is interpreted as judgmental. Besides, in our experience, the most common response by youth and adults alike is "I don't know." This leads to more frustration by the questioner and often elevates the discussion into a non-productive/non-restorative argument. Rather, by asking the first three questions, we already have begun to uncover their "Why" or, as Dr. Watlington describes it, their "private logic." We achieve the same end of receiving an explanation without the blockage of defensiveness and shutting down dialogue.

Additionally, these questions don't propel us into the philosophical debates of right and wrong. For instance, someone steals a cell phone, then trades it to someone else for money to pay for her portion of the rent. We normally spend important energy debating the rightness or wrongness of her actions, including a utilitarian philosophical argument about the lesser of two evils, or perhaps questioning her moral compass. We debate whether or not she knew right from wrong, whether stealing to take care of your basic needs in a class-based society is really wrong, and who determines what's a crime anyway. I've had too many of these conversations with colleagues and parents of students as we argue passionately about the rightness or wrongness of a particular incident. Because these conversations were anchored inside of the Punitive Paradigm, what was always missing was the more important questions of harm, needs, and repair. When using the Restorative Questions, we don't have to agree on whether their actions were inherently right or wrong, good or evil. This means that we also aren't required to judge whether they are good or bad as people. Instead, by acknowledging what occurred and then engaging in this process, we focus on the harm, which is, ultimately, most important. This is a powerful shift for those causing harm and for those of us trying to help.

Questions for Those Harmed/Impacted

As we've discussed, one of the real powerful benefits of the restorative approach over the punitive approach is the attention and support given to those harmed or impacted by the wrongdoing. Along with the questions we ask the wrongdoer, there are a set of questions to ask those who have been harmed. These include:

1. What happened?
2. What were you thinking when you realized what happened?
3. How have you and your loved ones been impacted?
4. What has been the hardest thing for you?
5. What needs to happen in order to make things right or better?

You'll notice that these questions mirror the original set, but let's dive into them a bit further.

What happened?

Again, this simple question gives those harmed a chance to tell their narrative, preventing us from assuming that we know everything that happened. This question offers the harmed party validation that their voice matters and that their experience is worthy of being shared. Also, often in the retelling, they get a chance to review the full scope of events, which sometimes includes how their behavior might have impacted the event.

What were you thinking when you realized what happened?

Similar to the antecedent question asked to the wrongdoer, this question begins to unpack some of the underlying thoughts and feelings of the person harmed. Sometimes they share their understanding of the root causes of the incident, including a reflection on any responsibility they might have as well. "I kept pushing even though I saw that she was getting frustrated; I just didn't expect her to hit me though." As we process the incident with them, these first two questions allow them to begin at the level of thoughts, and then we challenge by going deeper into the emotional level with the next two. At this question, we begin to uncover any unreconciled shame presenting as attacking other, attacking self, avoidance or withdrawal.

How have you and your loved ones been impacted?

When asking this question, the nuances of the incident are revealed. For example, let's consider a situation where an employer delivered employee paychecks a day late. The employer may have thought this was simply an inconvenience and frustration for the employee. Instead, when the employee answered this question, the employer learned that this caused her account to be overdrawn, thereby canceling her last payment for a surprise flight for her anniversary trip with her husband. This helps to further understand the ripple effect of the harm. Too often, these "ancillary" people are not considered.

Travel Notes from the Journey

"Malik, I believe they're going to sue us." That was the first thing that I heard when I picked up the call from our Regional Director. I knew immediately what he was referencing: a parent had recently pulled his child from our program and had contracted with an educational advocate. Often, the next thing to happen was an official letter notifying of a potential lawsuit. We didn't get many of these, but typically they would make my blood boil. But I was evolving in my Restorative practice, and I was convinced that I needed to have a conversation with the parent. It wasn't until I started dialing the number that I realized I could use the Restorative Questions for someone harmed here. His defenses were up when I began with "What happened?", but by the time I asked "What has been the hardest thing for you?" there were cracks in his voice. We didn't need to spend much time on the last Restorative Question. His need was clear: he wanted me to assure him that our staff would try harder to treat his son like I was treating him now, with an open heart and understanding. I was able to make that promise. He and his son returned to school the next day.

What has been the hardest thing for you?

With this question, we are essentially trying to get everything on the table. The healing process begins not when we remove the knife from the wound or cover it up with bandages, but when we provide antiseptic to clear the wound and prevent further infection. In other words, this question helps us provide the space and opportunity for those harmed to speak their truth. Most importantly, this uncovers their needs, which are essential to identify for restoration and leads us right into the last question.

What needs to happen to make things right or better?

By engaging in this process systematically, we have prepared those harmed for the repair question. That is, by this point, they have shared their narrative, explored their feelings and the impact on themselves and those they care about, and begun to identify their needs. Now, we begin to tackle what plan of action can be developed to repair and restore. In our experience, this question is as hard for those harmed as it is for those causing harm. Often, when people have been wronged, they are so used to being at an impasse or to being excluded from the outcomes that they don't know how to answer a question like this. That's okay. Let's be both patient and gently firm. Let's give them time and support in answering. Ultimately, we need to affirm that the conflict is theirs as well, and let them know they have the privilege and responsibility to share what needs to happen next.

The Least You Should Know

- When we lack the language to explain our emotions, we often channel our emotions into our behavior.
- Affective language is language that expresses affect, emotion, and feelings. Many people struggle to use affective language, particularly men and boys, who are trained by our culture not to express emotions. This can be especially true for men and boys of color.
- In Restorative Practices, affective language is both modeled and taught through Affective Statements and Restorative Questions.
- Affective Statements are "I" statements that express emotion and are connected to behavior. Most of us are good at using Affective Statements to express positive emotion but struggle to use them to express negative emotion.
- Restorative Questions are the key to helping a wrongdoer process the damage they caused and create an action plan to heal that damage. These questions also help you learn about the event without showing judgment.
- Restorative Questions can also be posed of the person harmed. These questions help them feel validated and begin to think through paths toward healing and restoration.

7 Circles to Connect and Heal

"Everything an Indian does is in a circle, and that is because the power of the World always works in circles, and everything tries to be round . . . The sky is round and I have heard the earth is round like a ball, and so are all the stars. The wind in its greatest power whirls, birds make their nest in circles, for theirs is the same religion as ours. The sun comes forth and goes down again in a circle. The moon does the same and both are round. Even the seasons form a great circle in their changing, and always come back again to where they were. Our teepees were round like the nests of birds. And they were always set in a circle, the nation's hoop." —Chief Black Elk

There is no single structure more characteristic of Restorative Practices than the Circle. It lives in the soul of this work. In fact, when we work with folks who have had some experience with Restorative Practices, the first thing they reference is how many Circles they are or are not conducting. My immediate response sounds like something Yoda would say: "A Circle does not restorative make." While something magical can happen when we simply sit in a Circle together, it is not necessarily guaranteed. Similarly, while Circles are heavily aligned with being Restorative, much of the most important work happens outside of them. However, the Circle remains a central and critical element in our Restorative Practices.

Many superb books have been written on the power and effectiveness of the Circle process in different settings, including *The Little Book of Circle Processes* by Kay Prannis, *Peacemaking Circles and Urban Youth* by Carolyn Boyes-Watson, and *Corporate Circles* by Maureen Fitzgerald. This chapter will share only some elements of the Circle that characterize how I have seen them used most effectively in Restorative Practices.

Philosophy of Circles

Let's start from the truth that circles are natural. Just like relationships and human connection are not only central but critical for us as social beings, circles are a natural way for us to connect and build those relationships. We gather in circles throughout all social settings and across cultures and socio-economic status. The huddle in American football, basketball, and other sports is an example of a natural circle. The stand-up team meeting is most often executed in a circle. More than two friends meeting together in a parking lot, store, or home form a natural circle to talk. Communal prayer across various religious traditions are sometimes done in circles, such as in the Mormon endowment ceremony, Muslims in prayer circulating the Kaaba, and Kateri Prayer Circles by some Native American Catholics. Collective dancing often takes place in circles. And many families share meals at a circular table.

In fact, we find circles throughout the cultural landscape of traditional societies, especially those with roots within Africa and Indigenous America. As I explore in more depth in *We Can Save Our Boys of Color*, it is critically important that anyone facilitating a Circle have cultural humility when discussing this practice with communities of color. This means we need to acknowledge the ancient roots of the Circle practice in these cultures. To not acknowledge this, and to state or imply that the Western or European world has created this model, is a form of cultural imperialism.

But why has the Circle stood the test of time as the preeminent vehicle for collective human connection? What does it provide for us that other models can't? It encourages engagement, promotes equality and equity, is inherently inclusive, creates trust and connection, and builds leaders. Let's explore each of these individually.

Engagement

In the Circle, everyone can be seen, literally. Ideally, there are no obstructions between people, meaning no desks, no tables, and no phones between participants. When we establish this norm within our Circles, the level of transparency and openness is heightened. There is no hiding behind our notebooks and screens, and there is no mental disconnection through the illusion of multitasking. Ultimately, when we are transparent in our body language, people stay more engaged!

A colleague and long-time Restorative Practitioner once told me about a Circle that he was facilitating with about thirty participants. Despite having established a norm that using cell phones during the Circle process was not allowed and would be considered rude, one participant kept taking out his phone in the middle of the Circle. Although he tried to be discreet and text using one hand with the phone at the side of his leg, everyone could see what he was doing. What made things worse was that he would then jump into the discussion to give folks the benefit of his opinion without having apparently paid much attention when they spoke.

After some time of this, with the group clearly looking towards my friend for direction, he pulled the phone-user aside. He said, "I'm not sure what's going on, but I'm pretty frustrated when you take out your cell phone and text while in the Circle. I'm asking you to either stop or leave the Circle to use your phone." Needless to say, the culprit apologized, put his phone away, and didn't take it out for the remainder of their time together. Not surprisingly, my friend described his demeanor as more engaging, with more active listening and less intrusive behavior, after his phone was put away. This is also a great example of the power of making an Affective Statement, even with someone that you don't know at all. The Circle, when facilitated well, promotes collective engagement and shared accountability.

Equality and Equity

When we believe in equality, we believe all people should be treated the same way. Equity takes this a step further by recognizing that not everyone starts out on equal footing; to make true equality happen, different people need different things. For example, equality means believing everyone should have an equal voice. Equity means recognizing that some people were born with loud voices, but we need to give others the assistance of a megaphone.

The Circle itself is a quintessential democratic structure that promotes equality and equity. The value of participation that underpins the Restorative Circle is exactly what we find within our most highly functioning organizations, classrooms, and communities. Here are a few ways the Restorative Circle promotes both equality and equity:

- Access to information: The Circle allows everyone to share equal access to information and input. Everyone can engage, interpret, and question knowledge on equal footing.
- Hierarchy: To truly achieve equity and collective input, we require a departure from typical Western hierarchical symbols. As Carolyn Boyes-Watson explains in her book

Peacemaking Circles and Urban Youth, the Circle is powerful because it doesn't include the traditional symbols of power and significance: No table to hide behind, no podium for power, no back of the room, no symbols of hierarchy. This is precisely what speaks most to youth who, by definition, are without power or position, therefore voice.

- All participants, no bystanders: As there is no "head" of the Circle, everyone, including the facilitator, are active participants. There are no bystanders or observers. If you are in the Circle, you participate.

In short, we use the Circle because it provides the opportunity to engage everyone. All participants in the Circle—students and teachers, children and parents, workers and managers, community members and leaders—have an equal voice and equal power. The Circle provides the literal and symbolic equity that aligns with the values of Restorative Practices.

Inclusion

In a recent Circle training with about ninety participants, I facilitated a brief sequential circle process (this structure is described later in this chapter), where everyone got a chance to sound off on how they felt about a particular topic. This is normal within our Restorative work, but certainly not normal within most trainings, meetings, classrooms, and families. The process only took about eight minutes but was a powerful indicator that all voices were valued. Participants were encouraged to speak as loudly as they could so that all voices could be heard and ideas shared. This, of course, was an extremely large circle and not ideal for inclusivity, yet it manifested. The beautiful thing about the Circle is that it reminds us to make space for all voices to be heard, both the "dominant" and "quiet" ones alike.

In my experience as a leader and educator, too many of our meetings are overtaken by the loudest and oft-heard voices. These are often the extroverts or those who process externally and share their thoughts frequently. We know that society has made this more acceptable for boys and men than it has for girls and women outside of the family context. Within our classrooms and meetings, male dominance, regardless of positional authority, can be seen in who interrupts and dominates the conversation most. As a man, I have been working hard to acknowledge and change this habit in myself.

> "Coming together is inevitable, community is intentional"
> –Steve Korr

However, when facilitated by the wise practitioner and embedded in a collective spirit of trust and emotional safety, the Circle can be a dynamic place where all voices can be heard. We have found that, within the Circle, it is so much easier to have focused attention on the person speaking. When the spirit and flow of dialogue becomes lopsided, the facilitator or collective helps to moderate contributions. It is starkly clear that the Circle is a bonafide approach to ensuring that we hear and value the voices of all.

Travel Notes from the Journey

It was January 2016 and I received five back-to-back text messages that one of our team members had just lost their house to a fire. Maria had lost everything, and she and her children were homeless. The texts came from the State Director who was frantically following protocol and trying to pull together material support for the family. As the vice president, I jumped in to see what resources I could bring to bear as well. This was what we did; we pulled together to support each other. But it dawned on me that something was missing here. I began to wonder if I was operating in the FOR box given that we hadn't initiated a plan WITH Maria herself. Within minutes we organized a "virtual Circle" using video conferencing to connect with her and about six key team members. We shared and learned a lot in those forty-five minutes, including that Maria was safe, had a semi-permanent place to stay, and had no immediate material needs. She also saw that her work family from near and far felt connected and impacted by what happened and valued the opportunity to hear from her directly. Tears fell, hers and ours. I learned that although it was going to feel great to give Maria things we thought she needed, it was especially meaningful to work through the challenges together in a Circle, even if I was hundreds of miles away.

Trust and Connection

The "magic" of the Circle does not start immediately with trust and connection. The "magic" is in holding the space for that to emerge on its own. By facilitating from a WITH approach and establishing norms that promote openness and respect, we foster authentic connection between participants. In this space, participants get an opportunity to have voice and bonding, where we get to see the humanity in each other, thus making it much harder to hurt and choose to violate each other. In this space, moral authority and empathy rule over titles, age, or other categories that create us and the "other."

I know, I know this sounds like a "pie-in-the-sky" scenario, which is exactly why many folks unfamiliar with the process write it off. However, let me share a personal story:

In early 2017, Akoben hosted a men's retreat with about ten participants over a weekend. Every element of these retreats is meticulously and intentionally planned to maximize our time together and foster both brotherhood and better human development. This includes individual time for meditation, competitive physical activities, collective meal preparation, and personal development workshops. This particular retreat was dynamic in that while all the participants were Black or Latino, it brought together men across a wide age spectrum and also cut across class, religion, profession, and other background demographics. It included people who don't often sit together as equals, including a lawyer, a former inmate, and several students. Woven throughout our time together were small- and whole-group Circles.

During our second night, we watched the movie *Moonlight*, pausing at three planned intervals to have a Circle discussion about the movie. We chose this powerful movie because it squarely challenges the viewer to confront complex notions of masculinity, trauma, sexual orientation, sexuality, family dysfunction, and brotherhood. Most of these men had not met prior to the weekend, and all of us brought our own baggage and historical challenges with life. Despite only having about twenty-four hours of relationship tenure with each other, the Circle that evening created a space where these brave men shared their ideas, frustrations, and fears around the issues raised by the movie. As you can imagine, these were not the easy issues, and we weren't having a quasi-intellectual debate over Michael Jordan vs Lebron James, Biggie vs Tupac, or anything else you might hear at the barbershop. Instead, we talked about subjects like fatherhood, Dubois' concept of double-consciousness, toxic masculinity, financial freedom, and commitment in intimate relationships. This Circle allowed us to push deeper, challenge each other more, and leave moved by others' contributions to our hearts and thinking. Trust and connection that didn't exist before were forged through the time put in the Circle.

Leadership

In the Circle, the leader isn't the most important voice. While the facilitator can contribute to and even guide the discussion when necessary, they also are a member of the greater collective. This is not to shirk leadership responsibility or abdicate positional authority, but quite the opposite: to leverage leadership by leaning into a process that builds other leaders around us. There are some great opportunities to encourage leadership in the Circle process, including:

- The first volunteer to respond determines the direction in a Sequential Circle.
- A talking piece is used, including for the facilitator, communicating that everyone is held accountable to the same norms.

- A participant determines the topic of the Circle.
- Someone other than the positional leader facilitates the Circle.

The Circle can create opportunities for small leadership moments that build the bench of emerging leaders. As we will explore later, the structure and process of the Circle are designed to promote individual and collective voice.

Structure of Restorative Circles

As we mentioned at the beginning of this chapter, the Circle is an ancient process, rooted within nearly every traditional culture. In fact, we often say that a circle is the most democratic way our ancient ancestors shared warmth around a fire. When we look at its use historically, we find that it is often the symbol of social equality and collective power. For instance, in the myth of King Arthur's Round Table, by placing each of the knights on equal footing, they would cease internal violence and disputes around status. Within the Iroquois People of the Longhouse, the Council of Clan Mothers would use the Circle process to empower the voice and leadership of women within the nation.

Over the years, our Akoben team's experiences with Restorative Circles have run the gamut of relationships and social interactions. One week we might facilitate a small, impromptu Circle with a leadership team to brainstorm a quick solution to a pressing problem. The next week, we might facilitate a multi-day Circle with community stakeholders to address institutional issues impacting the economy. No matter the size of the organization or the size of the problem, every organization benefits from the power of the Circle. In fact, we have yet to find a situation, critical or otherwise, involving more than two people (which nearly every situation does) that doesn't benefit from a Circle. While there are exceptions, including instances of intense harm (such as abuse, assault, and trauma), we have found that even these can benefit from a Circle between appropriate participants and at the appropriate time to, at the very least, support the healing process.

The particular use of the Circle determines the type of Circle. As we will discuss in the next section, there are a wide range of Circle processes, each powerful when used appropriately. To begin, let's look at three basic structural elements of the Circle: their duration, their size, and their shape.

Duration

There are no definitive time requirements for an effective Circle. We have conducted Circles that have barely lasted five minutes and those that have taken several days. The accepted understanding is that the participants and process determine the duration. As facilitators, we often tend to conduct the Circle within a time period that aligns with our schedules. With effective facilitation, which we will explore in the next section, we can foster the Restorative experience within that timeframe. However, sometimes our planning or facilitation doesn't align with the needs of the Circle participants. In this case, we must either adjust our schedule or adjust our expectations of "closure" for the moment. Like humans themselves, the Circle is an organic and dynamic process that has its own time and tempo. Experience and skill level help in modifying those to our needs.

The time required for a Circle is also dependent on the purpose. In general, we have found that Proactive Circles are shorter than Responsive Circles. Proactive Circles, which are designed to build community and rapport between participants, usually take between a few minutes to less than an hour. Responsive Circles, which are Circles called in order to address a specific issue, take longer, as these typically require more than just Affective Statements but often collective discussion using the Restorative Questions.

When planning the time for a Responsive Circle, be sure to adhere to some general best practices of engagement, including the following:

- Allow for regular breaks (at least 5-10 minutes each hour).
- Be attuned to the body language and frustration level of participants. This helps you know when to call a break or when it's necessary to stay in the space of discomfort for growth and restoration.
- Conclude on time, or else explicitly ask for consensus for a specific extension of time.
- It's okay to not have closure. You can call for a continuation of the Circle later.

Size

Like time requirements, the size of the Circle is not static either. At a minimum, a Circle consists of at least three people, including the facilitator. However, on the top end, there really is no limit. My colleagues and I frequently participate in and facilitate Circles with more than 100 participants. At times, we have held concentric circles in tight rooms to fit everyone. I have enjoyed participating in a range of Circles myself, from a powerful Circle with just three of us around a campfire in northern Arizona, to a learning Circle with 150 participants at a global martial arts conference in Toronto, Canada. The process itself is flexible enough to meet our needs when planned well.

With that said, optimally, you want to organize the Circle with between five and twenty-five participants depending on the purpose and topic. This appears to be the "sweet spot" for maximum engagement in proactive and responsive Circles. An experienced facilitator can effectively handle more, but we use a ratio of 1:50 in most of our Circles with advanced facilitators depending on the intensity of the topic or severity of harm.

Shape

I'll say something here that may sound funny: In order to reap the full benefits of a Circle, it needs to be a circle.

Yes, the shape of the structure matters. In fact, I have one close colleague who obsesses a bit over the shape of the Circle, giving close attention to the precise positioning of chairs before the process begins and holding participants accountable to maintaining the integrity of the Circle's shape. When I teased him about it, he reminded me that this is an intentional space where serious work towards building or repairing

> **"The reason the Oval Office is round is there are no corners you can hide in."**
> **—attributed to George W. Bush**

relationships is accomplished. We need to treat it with the respect that it deserves and guide others to do the same. I agree. When we focus on the fact that we are explicitly choosing to sit in a circle, we should maximize the benefits of doing so by attending to the shape.

What happens when we encounter limitations to setting up a perfect circle? When we don't have the luxury of cooperative furniture or a big open space? The answer is simple: We hold the Circle anyway. I'm fond of sharing the following with folks:

A circle is better than an oval.
An oval is better than a square.
A square is better than a rectangle.
A rectangle is better than an "L" shape.
An "L" shape is better than nothing.

The message is clear: In the absence of a perfect circle, you still hold the Circle. While the sanctity of the shape is important, the Circle mindset is more important than the Circle shape. Approaching the process with the Restorative mindset, facilitating from that mindset, and allowing the process to be organically experienced by those within the Circle is much more powerful than getting frustrated over the perfect layout of the chairs. Therefore, we have no excuses based on furniture, room layout, or space.

At the same time, when we push ourselves to adhere to the shape requirements of the Circle, we unleash our creativity. We can begin thinking about space more flexibly and move beyond the challenges we initially notice.

For instance, while coaching a team of teachers in a challenging Philadelphia high school a few years ago, I had been asked by some naysayers to demonstrate a Circle with students in a math class on the spur of the moment. Normally, doing this either puts me in the FOR box of doing the heavy lifting for them or isn't always helpful for them to discover their own facilitation style. However, this time I resisted my inclination to push back and instead jumped into the opportunity.

As you can imagine, when we arrived at the classroom, the desks were in traditional rows, about twenty students were just arriving, and we only had about ten minutes for the activity. I had about twenty seconds during the teacher's introduction to figure out what we would do. I knew I couldn't take precious time moving furniture or I would lose the students' attention in the chaos. After greeting them briefly, I asked them to stand up quickly and do something that is unusual. I suggested we sit on the desks in a circle! After getting a few strange looks from the students and observing adults, the students agreed to the proposition. They looked uncomfortable at first, probably because they were not used to being allowed to sit on desks, some had to share desktop space, and because, well, sitting on a desk can be uncomfortable! But they seemed to be okay when I joined them in the makeshift Circle and especially liked it when I told the adults in the room they had to join in as well.

We did two quick rounds using a sequential circle. One question, "How do you spell your name?" was just an interesting way to introduce ourselves. The second question, "What was your favorite lesson or unit so far this year?" was to push a little deeper to get substantive feedback on the students' learning experience. Once we concluded, I thanked everyone for participating, and the young people assumed their normal positions at theirs desk and launched into their lesson. As we were leaving, I remember one young lady calling out: "Hey Mr. M.,

> ~Travel Tip~
> Don't worry too much about moving furniture when you're just starting out. Get folks up and hold a standing circle for a few minutes. They will appreciate the physical movement and you'll realize that forming a circle isn't as hard as you might think.

do you think that we can do that again sometime?" I looked at the other adults and said, "I'm pretty sure that we can."

Types of Circles

I'd like to give credit here again to the International Institute for Restorative Practices for their contribution to the field in conceptualizing and teaching various Circle processes. They have done tremendous work in popularizing both Proactive or Responsive Circles. Proactive Circles are those designed to build social capital and relationships, establish connections in the community, teach, etc. In Restorative environments, such Circles are a mainstay of how folks do their work and normal business. Responsive Circles, on the other hand, are held in connection to an event or challenge. They explore, unpack, and seek to resolve harm with as many impacted participants as possible.

If you are using Circles in your school, community, workplace, or home, we encourage you to make about eighty percent of Circles Proactive and twenty percent Responsive. Using Circles proactively helps build connections in order to minimize future wrongdoing. When wrongdoing does happen, the connections built through Proactive Circles can help minimize the harm done and resolve it more quickly.

The structural type of Circles held are either Sequential, Non-Sequential, or Fishbowl. Let's look at each here:

Sequential Circle

In my experience, the Sequential Circle is undoubtedly the most used type of Circle for beginners and advanced practitioners alike. This is probably due to its ease of understanding and implementation. We intuitively understand the norms of a Sequential Circle. The person who speaks next is just the next one in line. There appears to be a democracy about this, that regardless of where you are sitting or standing in the Circle, you know when your turn is coming. Some love it, some dread it, but almost everyone understands it.

Sequential	Also called a "Go-Around." By far the most commonly used Circle, especially for beginners. This simple process rotates input clockwise or counterclockwise around the circle.	
Non-Sequential	Also called a "Popcorn Circle." A common structure to elevate the level of risk within the group, allowing for varying levels of participation.	
Fishbowl	Also called a "Processing Circle." A specialized structure design to have an inner circle of active participants and an outer circle of active observers	

Another benefit of the Sequential Circle is that it ensures all participants have an opportunity to share. When conducted well, this Circle allows for all voices to be heard, even if a few choose to "pass." Whether in a meeting, classroom, or family Circle, when we use the sequential process, we are setting the expectation and opportunity for all participants to contribute.

That being said, the Sequential Circle presents its share of challenges. The two most significant challenges include adequate preparation and appropriate facilitation. Where many of us run into difficulty when conducting a Sequential Circle is in developing quality questions. Given that we are seeking the collective input from all present, the stakes are higher that we facilitate a worthy process. In other words, we must take the time to develop powerful low-, medium-, or high-risk questions that fit the group and are designed to achieve both connection and challenge. In a very real sense, the power of the Circle is in the power of the questions asked.

The other challenge occurs with ensuring that we use the appropriate facilitation style to modulate pacing and participation. For the Sequential Circle, our aims are often to keep the energy moving and provide for collective input. While this holds true for the other Circle types, we are most interested in the democracy and equity of the Sequential Circle. It is most important that *everyone* has the opportunity to share; therefore, as a facilitator we must focus on pacing and participation. By providing the space for all voices to be heard, we are focusing on connection; by keeping the norms around participation and pacing, we are making room for challenge. We accomplish the latter by establishing and reestablishing the ground rules for engagement, including who speaks when and for how long, which challenges both those who normally don't talk and those who would otherwise "overtalk."

Once, I was facilitating a training with leaders in upstate New York. To initiate the training, I launched into a normal Sequential Circle and prompted introductions. Most of the participants knew each other, so this was designed to be a quick sharing of each person's name, organization, and one word to describe how they were feeling that morning. I had mentally allotted eight minutes for the process with about forty-five participants and gave them brief directions for what to do. I noticed that one participant had not been paying attention and was talking throughout the directions, so, in my naiveté and a little of my TO box default, I asked him to start off the process.

Clearly, the man had not heard my directions. He immediately jumped up, placed himself in the center of the circle, and launched into a Shakespearean introduction of his ancestry, backstory, and philosophy of life. And he did it all in Tagalog, his native language of the Philippines! It was both beautiful and frustrating because this took him about five minutes, without pausing for breath or a natural place for me to interrupt him. Once satisfied that he had conveyed his message in his indigenous tongue, he then translated everything that he had said into English for our understanding. Of course, it helped that his journey and background were powerful. The challenge was that it had taken up all eight minutes! During his speech, while some clapped and seemed engaged, many had been looking at me as the facilitator with both empathy and frustration. Once the man sat down, I thanked him deeply for sharing such a personal introduction. I praised

~Travel Tip~

It is important to acknowledge that cultural norms play a role in how we introduce ourselves. The facilitator needs to be aware of those norms if they are facilitating with a group of people who are largely from a culture not the facilitator's own.

him for starting us off on the right foot with getting vulnerable and modeling the way. However, I raised that he had not followed our norms and the impact was that this affected everyone else's time to share. I explained that by doing what he did, he placed himself above everyone else. Many in the Circle nodded their heads, and some showed an affect of concern. However, in that moment, all probably understood that I was going to take facilitating through connection and challenge pretty seriously. He apologized to the collective. We did the remaining introductions in about seven minutes and worked through our scheduled morning break! At lunch, he and I ate together and bonded around the similarities of our personal stories.

Non-Sequential Circle

The Non-Sequential Circle is dynamic, building off of the energy of the room and allowing leaders to shine.

We often use this type of circle to dive deeper into an issue, raising the level of emotional risk and connection. This type of Circle is powerful because it mirrors a natural conversation within a group. While the Sequential Circle is poignant in its simplicity and intentional structure, sometimes it can feel forced and artificial in how it expects everyone to participate. The Non-Sequential Circle feels different in that it allows folks to jump in as they feel moved. This process reminds me of the image of a young girl playing double-dutch, where her body is swaying back

~Travel Tip~

It is best practice to use a talking piece, especially when holding a non-sequential circle. The talking piece is a physical symbol of respecting the voice sharing at the moment. My favorite talking piece is a small replica djembe (African drum). It has significance both culturally and personally. Identify a talking piece that has meaning for you and your community as well.

and forth with the rhythm of the rope, trying to find just the right time to jump in. The Non-Sequential Circle is similar in that it produces energy and flows. It also helps to capture and build off of the ideas of others in real-time, rather than forcing participants to wait for their turns around the Circle to comment.

However, the Non-Sequential Circle has its challenges as well. When participants have the ability to respond immediately to another's comments or have their own comment either praised or critiqued, this can create the space for defensiveness, judgement, and a lack of emotional safety. This also allows the loudest voices to dominate the discussion, often with more personal storytelling than necessary or appropriate. Strong facilitation, including the use of a talking piece and respectful interruption when appropriate, is frequently necessary with the Non-Sequential Circle.

Fishbowl Circle

The Fishbowl is probably the least used among these three types of Circles, although it can be incredibly effective in achieving collective input for problem-solving or maximizing the participation of a large number of people.

To facilitate a Fishbowl Circle, follow these steps:

1. Organize the larger group into an outer Circle.
2. Determine how many volunteers you need using a 1:5 ratio (one volunteer for every five participants).
3. Ask for the volunteers to bring their chairs and join you in the center of the Circle. Arrange these chairs in a circle.
4. Set up empty chair(s) as part of the inner Circle. Use the same 1:5 ratio (one empty chair for every five volunteers).
5. Explain that we will do a Sequential or Non-Sequential Circle in the inside Circle. The empty chairs are opportunities for the active observers on the outside to temporarily join the conversation.

With an inner Circle of active participants and an outer Circle of active observers, this process creates expectations and opportunities for input from all. The great thing about the Fishbowl Circle is that it provides for the ability to have a real experience for those on the inside and virtual experience for those on the outside. It takes significantly less spatial movement than trying to organize smaller circles for the entire large group. It also allows for the facilitator to leverage the energy of volunteers to participate while creating opportunities via the empty chair(s) for others to jump in as the spirit moves them.

> "Draw a circle around yourself – invite people in or keep them out. We are the creators of our social geometry. Calculate your volume."
> –Rachel Wolchin

The challenges of the Fishbowl Circle are related to the quality of the questions posed to the inner Circle. Where I have struggled in the past is when I didn't have a powerful enough question for the group. In those situations, the inner Circle breezes through the dialogue too quickly, which limits the amount of time those in the outer Circle have to process and possibly jump into the inner conversation. I've learned that good preparation is required to effectively capture the dynamic energy of the volunteers who are eager to participate and can make the experience much richer if given the opportunity. Also, the facilitator must ensure that quiet voices and participants are given the chance to share as well.

Personalizing Your Circles

While nearly all practitioners weave their own personalities into the Circle process, naturally some practitioners are more prescriptive than others. As you can imagine, some practitioners are more dogmatic about strict adherence to their way of conducting Circles, standardizing and enforcing who does what, which direction the conversation flows, and what norms are established. Others provide so much freedom in implementation that they hardly look like a bonafide Circle structure at all. If not careful, both of these can be errors manifesting a TO or FOR approach.

Throughout the years, we have learned and shared experiences with effectively facilitating Circles with thousands of practitioners around the globe. Some of the most important questions to think about include:

- When is it appropriate to use the Circle?
- How does the facilitator maintain a WITH mentality during the process?
- What does emotional safety look like in the Circle?
- What norms should we establish and how many?
- What happens when trauma shows up in the Circle?
- How can we weave rituals into the Circle process?
- When should we use a talking piece and how?
- How do we find time to hold Circles?
- What are the best practices in Sequential, Non-Sequential, and Fishbowl Circles?

Handling each of these is outside the scope of this book. However, we will be releasing another book exclusively dedicated to the use of Restorative Circles. In the meantime, I encourage you to tackle these questions in your own specific context with the people involved in your Circles.

The Least You Should Know

- Circles are a natural, ancient, and powerful structure to foster change through connection and challenge.
- Circles encourage engagement, promote equity and equality, are inherently inclusive, create trust and connection, and build leaders.
- Circles can vary greatly in size and duration, depending on the needs of the situation.
- Circles can be proactive or responsive.
- Structurally, circles can be Sequential, Non-Sequential, or Fishbowl.

Part Three: Reflection

"Learning without reflection is a waste. Reflection without learning is dangerous." —Confucius

"True progress means matching the world to the vision in our heads but we always change the vision instead."
— "Circles" by rock band Thrice

8   Excuse Me, but I Have A Question!

"I would rather have questions that can't be answered than answers that can't be questioned." —Richard Feynman

"Courage doesn't happen when you have all the answers. It happens when you are ready to face the questions you have been avoiding your whole life." —Shannon L. Alder

In our trainings, we grant people permission to ask their questions throughout the day, to not hesitate or wait until a Q&A period. We also encourage them to ask their most challenging questions because this work is just too important to get wrong! We are all learning together on this Restorative Journey.

I've compiled some of the most commonly asked questions below. Our hope is that these questions and initial responses will help guide us in pushing even more deeply into the theory and practice of this work.

Here we go:

What practical skills are most important in Restorative Practices?

While the Restorative theory and framework is critically important (and a priority before learning any practical Restorative skills), taking action is a necessity. By reading this book, you should be prepared to do at least a few practical things:

1.   Apply the Social Discipline Window to analyze your use of authority.
2.   Immediately begin using Affective Statements.
3.   Immediately begin using Restorative Questions.
4.   Begin experimenting with Proactive Circles.

Of course, a book is not a substitute for in-person training, where we explore each of these more deeply with interactive activities and hands-on coaching. However, you are well underway in launching your Restorative Journey by implementing these four skills above.

What if I have to implement the punitive approach due to my organization's policies and expectations?

Most institutions naturally require some version of the punitive approach given that it is so dominant in our society. However, we have found that the shift is happening away from the most prescriptive and required responses to more nuanced and discretionary responses. In that case, we often have more agency than we think to implement Restorative Practices. Even if you are in an environment that is dogmatic around the use of punishment, there are a few opportunities for you, including:

- The punitive paradigm is naturally a reactive one and doesn't help you build relationships and a positive culture. Therefore, there's an opportunity to leverage your Restorative Practices for proactively building community and social capital outside of responses to wrongdoing. For example, you could make Proactive Circles part of your staff meetings or weave Affective Statements into your normal dialogue with coworkers or those you serve.

- Be open and honest, and educate those with positional authority that you are on the Restorative Journey to understand and implement these practices. Let them know how excited you are about the opportunity to try something different, and ask for their support and encouragement. Don't ask to "pilot" it, as that might lead them to evaluate your success too early, when you are still in learning mode. Instead, offer to build the prototype; that is, start with a small model to learn, build, and test before wider implementation and formal evaluation.

- Lastly, determine where your line of rebellion will be. We all have one. Determine what you are willing to struggle for and sacrifice when pushing against a machine that you believe is hindering what is in the best interest of those you serve. Sometimes we have to be rebels!

Can the punitive and Restorative Paradigms co-exist? In other words, can we have our feet in both worlds at the same time?

The short answer is yes, at least for a time! Since most of our institutions, families, and the broader society are structured around the punitive model, we will always be on some part of the continuum between the two paradigms. Therefore, even if we decided to go full-speed ahead and implement the Restorative model 100%, we would continue to run parallel processes, even if unofficially, during the transition. And that is okay. There is often value in our current processes for sure, and implementing the Restorative model is hard work. Therefore, we often find ourselves implementing a hybrid of both systems for some time. Beware, though; this is often untenable, as adherents of both models will continue to challenge the process until a decision around direction is fully and explicitly made.

Don't all boxes in the Social Discipline Window work? Don't our people/students/staff need for us to vary our approaches?

By far, this is the most common question asked in our trainings around the Social Discipline Window! A variation of this question comes up every time, probably because it speaks to both our deeper need to understand the practical application of the model as well as sometimes a little bit of our own defensiveness around which box we typically find ourselves in. I always smile when it comes up, because it seems like an old friend at this point.

In short, the answer is "sort of." I hope that you are smiling at that, too.

When we think about each box, let's consider possible uses and situations when the approach might be necessary:

- NOT Box: Honestly, I've yet to realize a situation when this is the most appropriate approach. When interfacing with those we have authority with, it doesn't seem that the approach of NO/LOW challenge and NO/LOW connection is effective at all. Even when we need to let someone "learn a lesson the hard way," we usually have established particular ranges of behavior or boundaries for them and ourselves (challenge) and let them know that we will be here for them when they want to do better (connection). That approach falls more appropriately within the WITH box.

- TO Box: The approach of HIGH challenge and LOW connection seems only appropriate in the face of a physically dangerous situation or crisis. When there is a fire, an active shooter, or a fight, for example, then those in authority have the responsibility to act with decisiveness in order to ensure safety. We don't pause for a vote, and we can't stop to give hugs or wipe away tears because we have a greater responsibility to keep people safe given the threat or reality of violence. However, we have a personal and collective responsibility not to misread situations. For example, for some people, the mere presence of children of color in an urban school equates to violence and physical danger; therefore, they justify their use of the TO box. This is obviously the intersection of their own biased logic and comfort with the TO box approach.

- FOR Box: We naturally default to the HIGH connection, LOW challenge approach of the FOR box when we are dealing with intense emotional pain. When someone is facing trauma, mourning the loss of a loved one, or struggling with another situation of emotional pain, our hearts naturally guide us to supporting them with love, encouragement, and compassion. This may mean that we forgive the profanity they are using or other forms of acting out in the moment. We find ourselves consoling them instead of correcting them. This is usually our instinctive reaction, and I believe it's the right one as long as we limit this response to an appropriate amount of time.

- WITH Box: We've made the argument for the WITH Box approach in Chapter 4. If I can't think of a situation when it's appropriate to use the NOT box, I'm also equally certain that the WITH box approach is universally appropriate. Even in the situations described above justifying the use of the TO and FOR boxes, those moments are temporary and must be anchored within a broader WITH approach. In other words, after the physical danger, we move quickly from TO back into the WITH box; after the person in intense emotional pain regulates, we move quickly from FOR back into the WITH box.

I'm a TO but I work with or am married to a FOR. Doesn't this work because we balance each other out?

Thank God for those who work with us! Whether it's in schools, companies, or families, it is a wonderful thing to have folks who help to balance us out and make sure we don't go too far into the deep end. If they are a TO and I'm a FOR, then we are good, right? Well, here are a few problems with this idea of "balancing each other out":

- Excuse for stagnation: What we have seen is that we can often use the existence of the other approaches as an excuse to not challenge our own TO, FOR, or NOT approaches. We count on them to give support because we are a good "hammer." Or, we need for them to enforce the rules, because we tend to the hearts of the family. This becomes a way to justify staying in our comfort zone.

- Taking advantage: When we settle into our TO/FOR corners and depend on the opposite approach by our partner or colleague, then we can absolutely find ourselves consistently taking advantage of them. What happens when the TO person doesn't always want to be the "bad guy," or the FOR person runs into compassion fatigue? We have trapped them, and ourselves, into one specific type of relationship with the people we serve, even when that relationship may not be in anyone's best interest.

- Ill-equipped for absence: When we rely on our partner for balance and let ourselves default to our comfort zone, what happens when you or they are absent? As I wrote in Chapter Three, when it comes to parenting, I used to rely on my wife's FOR approach to balance out my own TO approach. This changed when I realized it was risky for my kids to have only one parent operating from a place of high support. Now, my wife and I work hard to both operate from the WITH box.

I don't have enough time for this! How do I handle this when I don't have enough time to do everything already on my plate?

This question is an excellent one! It is most often asked by good-natured and well intentioned people who really believe in the principles of Restorative Practices. They understand the importance of connection and relationships and want to build them with colleagues, family members, students, and other people in their communities. They are simply faced with the restrictions of time. I offer two responses for the challenge of time.

First, when we deal with repairing harm or confronting wrongdoing, we have a choice between spending our time on the hard, often protracted work of doing it Restoratively or in the repetitive process of punishment. The Restorative work is the slow-burn process of building social capital on the front end so that people will be less likely to cause harm, and then processing and healing that harm when it does happen. The punitive approach appears expedient on face value, except it doesn't address root causes, respond to needs, or repair relationships. Therefore, the approach itself creates the cycle discussed in Chapter Two, where negative behavior leads to punishment, which leads to disconnectedness, which leads to more negative behavior. Therefore, the time that we spend in this cycle eats away not only at our time, but also at our relationship with the person being punished and at our own spirit. In the long run, the Restorative approach actually saves time and—even more importantly—strengthens your relationships.

Second, the best way that we can "master time and space" is to replicate ourselves. In other words, let's stop believing that we have to carry the entire weight of implementing this work by ourselves.

Yes, we can spark the launch. Yes, we may carry the torch and help others understand the path. However, ultimately, our greatest work occurs when we inspire others and help them begin their Restorative Journey as well. This includes those that we serve. We can master time and space when we have others also making Affective Statements, facilitating Circles, and using the Social Discipline Window to analyze their use of authority. All roads don't have to lead back to you as the "Restorative Answer!" I believe that being the spark and example of someone on the journey is powerful in itself.

Does this stuff work with my population? They are _____(fill in the blank: preschoolers, adults, urban youth, rural youth, challenging youth, incarcerated, special needs, executives, etc.)

If we are referring to whether or not this "Restorative stuff" works with various populations to help solve problems, repair relationships, and hold people accountable, then yes, it works! If we are referring to building a stronger sense of community in the classroom, neighborhood, family, workplace, or even prison in order to improve relationships and establish a sense of value, then yes, it works!

In all of our work, across every spectrum, age-group, and industry, we have yet to uncover a situation that could not benefit from being more Restorative. While some environments are more unusual or complicated and might require more creativity in implementation, the core principles discussed in this book are adaptable enough for every population. For instance, I was once asked by a very skeptical participant how Affective Statements might apply to her students, who are non-verbal and on the autism spectrum. I admitted that I certainly don't have expertise in this area, which prompted her to lean back, cross her arms, and smile with a satisfied "gotcha" look on her face. I then asked her, "Given your expertise with serving these students, how do you teach them to ask to use the bathroom or to show that they didn't do their homework?" She leaned forward, engaged again, and ran down a whole set of techniques from flashcards to hand signals that communicated a wide range of messages. I pointed out that these were probably the same instructional methods that she might use to introduce and wield Affective Statements with them as well. She got it and gave me a thumbs up. I smiled, leaned back, crossed my arms, and gave her a satisfied "gotcha" look!

9 Learning Together: Book Study Group Questions

"If you want to go fast, go alone. If you want to go far, go together."
—African proverb

The Restorative Journey is not done alone. The very nature of the WITH box requires us to be engaged fully in relationships with others. It is through these relationships with colleagues, peers, family, and those that we serve that we can teach and learn, be held accountable and supported, be challenged and connected. Reading this book with others is a fantastic way to deepen your understanding and implementation of this work. Here are some discussion questions to consider:

Chapter One

1. We describe a situation where we experienced success but didn't have a guiding theory or framework to explain why or how. Have you ever experienced this?

2. How is having a clear guiding theory or framework important to achieve or maintain success?

Chapter Two

1. Why does the Restorative mindset precede the teaching of restorative skills? Is the paradigm shift (the WHY) necessary before we start focusing on the skills (the HOW)?

2. How does the Punitive Model relate to the criminal justice system? What are its benefits, weaknesses, and potential outcomes?

3. How does the Restorative Model relate to highly functional family systems? What are its benefits, weaknesses, and potential outcomes?

4. Why should 80% of our restorative practices work be proactive and only 20% responsive?

Chapter Three

1. Discuss the formula Connection + Challenge = Change. How does this look in your organization and for you personally?

2. What does authentic connection look like as compared to superficial connection? What do they each accomplish?

3. How does connection relate to trauma-informed care?

4. What is social capital and why is it so important?

Chapter Four

1. Vulnerability is difficult for many of us. Why are we challenged with being vulnerable with those that we serve or are in relationships with? What can being vulnerable do to improve those relationships? How does our being vulnerable model for others to do the same?

2. Discuss the "Cycle of Disconnectedness."

3. Describe some popular characters that exemplify each of the boxes in the Social Discipline Window (e.g. Joe Clark from Lean On Me for the TO Box).

4. What box do you find yourself in most of the time with those you serve? With staff? At home? How about the approach of your supervisor?

5. How does a person's real or perceived seniority (job title, age, etc.) impact expectations around which box people operate from?

6. How does gender impact expectations around which box people operate from?

7. Discuss how the boxes relate to the concepts of Lose/Lose, Win/Lose, Lose/Win, and Win/Win.

8. How does the TO box approach, when taken to the extreme, relate to abuse and mass incarceration?

9. How does the FOR box approach, when taken to the extreme, relate to learned helplessness?

10. Discuss the table "Motivations for Each Box."

Chapter Five

1. What is stigmatizing shame? How does it relate to labeling, disconnection, and more harm?

2. What is reintegrative shame? How can it help process or manage shame restoratively?

3. Discuss the Compass of Shame and how you see it manifest in your setting.

Chapter Six

1. What is meant by an "emotional vocabulary" and a "behavioral vocabulary?" How do they relate to each other?

2. How is emotional vocabulary influenced by societal norms for gender, race, and ethnicity?

3. What are the three key ingredients for an Affective Statement? Discuss why all three are important.

4. Give some examples of Affective Statements and discuss

what is being communicated to the recipient for each one.

5. How does the "Story of Travis" reflect the power of Affective Statements?

6. What are the Restorative Questions? Discuss how each one is important to the process of repairing harm.

7. Think about the order of the questions. How does their sequence build the conversation toward accountability?

Chapter Seven

1. How are circles a natural structure in traditional and modern societies? What are other examples of using Circles outside of Restorative Practices?

2. Discuss how Circles promote engagement, inclusion, trust/connection, and leadership.

3. What structural elements of the Restorative Circle are most important for you?

4. When might you use the Sequential, Non-Sequential, or Fishbowl Circle?

5. The most common objection to implementing Circles is limited time. How would you overcome this objection? How do we find the time to do them?

10 Taking This to the Next Level

"The knowledge I have now is not the knowledge I had then."
—Kwame Ture

We owe a great debt and appreciation to our colleagues within the Restorative Practices movement for championing and broadening the use of these powerful practices, including Affective Statements and Circles, within schools and beyond. We have learned from, struggled alongside, and immersed ourselves with them for many years now.

Steve Korr, a colleague mentioned throughout the book, often states that the IQ around Restorative Practices has been increasing for years and that our level of analysis must keep pace. I interpret that to mean that, over time, the principles shared in this book have begun picking up steam within several fields. "Restorative Practices" as an idea is becoming popular. Therefore, those of us in the space of teaching these ideas must sharpen our analysis and be prepared to deepen the discussion. I agree with Steve. If people have learned the "ABCs" of this work, how do we move towards the construction of words, complex sentences, and ultimately deep, meaningful paragraphs?

In this last chapter I will provide a glimpse of a few areas where we can and should begin exploring more deeply into the theory and application of Restorative Practices. We delve into many of these topics in our workshops, and I will provide a richer analysis in subsequent books in this series. For now, here is a preview of where I believe this work should evolve.

Restorative Practices as Social Justice

The kind of practices that were laid out in this book encourage, maybe even require, us to reimagine our schools, workplaces, families, leadership, communities, and ourselves. As we engage more consciously in using our authority through the WITH box, we become keenly aware of how the TO, FOR, and NOT boxes are used and who they are used towards. In other words, when we approach this work honestly, it will require us to overtly confront issues of power, oppression, racism, sexism, classism, ableism, white privilege, male privilege, sexual orientation privilege, and other forms of prejudice and privilege.

Teaching Restorative skills is not enough if we don't also challenge our training participants to confront their own biases. The tools are both supportive to connect with those we are in relationship with but also challenging for ourselves to implement. Restorative Practices should not be able to neatly fit into hierarchical structures at work, home, schools, and communities. They should in fact question, denounce, and ultimately transform the principles of those hierarchical structures whenever those principles perpetuate inequity and marginalization.

The challenge for us is to sharpen our Restorative Practices as tools of equity and liberation, rather than simply dulling the negative effects of oppression.

To do that, we are going to have to get more comfortable as practitioners in weaving an analysis of power, privilege, and bias into our Restorative work.

Seek Harmony with Other Initiatives

I've had the opportunity to work in and with many organizations, both large and small. Inevitably, there comes a point where leadership has overloaded the organization with initiatives. This sometimes looks like a "new thing of the month club" where there is a surge of energy around a new idea, committees are formed, money is spent, and then something else new is introduced. As leaders and change agents, I believe that we have a serious responsibility to find the harmony between the initiatives we launch. We need to identify, or at the very least discuss, how these important things fit and work together.

Implementing Restorative Practices is no different. Within the school context, how does this work connect to your multi-tiered systems of support (MTSS) or positive behavior interventions systems (PBIS)? In workplaces, how do these practices interact with your protocols on sexual harassment and progressive discipline? At home, how does the social discipline window harmonize with your practice of giving allowance?

Recently in California I facilitated a full-day workshop exploring the intersection of Restorative Practices, bullying, law enforcement, and trauma. Participants were mainly educational leaders in districts where there were initiatives related to each of these areas, and they were interested to understand how they fit together. We spent the day "cross-mapping" these programs. Here are some collective discoveries:

- Deeper levels of understanding were achieved when we overlaid the Social Discipline Window to their previous trauma-informed care training to explain what boxes induce and exacerbate trauma.

- The Compass of Shame can help shed light on the causes of bullying behavior and possible Restorative solutions.

- Incorporating school police officers into Restorative Circles might positively shift the collective tone from crime to harm.

As this work evolves, the connection between Restorative Practices and other initiatives should become more explicit and clear.

Finding Indigenous Examples and Voices

As I mentioned earlier, the Circle is an ancient practice embedded in many indigenous communities around the world. We also can find examples of Affective Language in how many non-Western communities confront harm and wield reintegrative shame. These communities have been doing a variation of Restorative Practices long before others created this term for it.

Many of our colleagues in the Restorative Justice movement have championed an emphasis on including the voices of the First Nation and Indigenous people of the Americas. Examples of peacemaking Circles and Native understanding of harm versus crime are found throughout the literature, conferences, and regular practice. I worry that too often this is another illustration of the type of cultural appropriation and romanticizing of Native culture we find regularly in the West. All of us non-Natives benefiting from U.S. society today must be careful to not be disingenuous in the promulgation of cultural practices of a people whose genocide enabled the creation of the United States as we know it. Americans of European descent, whose ancestors committed this genocide and who today continue to benefit the most from it due to privilege, must be especially cognizant of this.

Further, there are also rich traditions found everywhere from indigenous communities that are rooted in what we call Restorative Practices or Justice. For instance, in Japan, "jidan" is a traditionally informal process of apologizing and making amends. Among the Lando people in Uganda, the ritual of "onyo pii" is done by pouring cold water on conflicted parties who wish to cool down and restore the relationship. Lastly, as I will describe in more detail in a subsequent book, the cipher is a Circle structure born of the desire of black and brown youth in the U.S. to connect and challenge each other through the medium of hip hop.

Our challenge is to have eyes open enough to see how this work has roots and continues to live within the cultures of different peoples around the world, especially marginalized communities. We can do this most effectively by engaging the populations most impacted by injustice and harm and listening to and valuing their wisdom and experiences.

This Work Belongs to the People

In Chapter Eight, I addressed the very common challenge of time. I raised that we can "master time and space" when we replicate ourselves. That is, when we teach and widen the circle so that others can understand and implement this work alongside us. To effectively do this we will need to resist the over-professionalization of Restorative Practices.

Restorative Practices has been described as an emerging social science. I like this idea, as it anchors what we have been doing now on a continuum, or journey, of deeper understanding of this work. However, "social science" is academic and research-based language. Certain things are valued above others in academia, including standards, data, written language, scripting, and credentialing. These are not, in themselves, problematic. However, when they are the only points of value, then other aspects of Restorative Practices are marginalized, including story sharing, flexibility, oral language, and community norms. These informal, non-academic aspects of this work help widen the circle of involvement to include anyone interested in living and working in a more Restorative culture, including people who don't have access to professional certification programs, such as youth, people whose jobs don't include professional development funds, low-income community members, and people wanting to implement this work within their families.

As we evolve as practitioners, we will need to navigate the pressure for more data, stronger definitions, standards, and external validation that "this stuff works." We will need to balance those pressures with the human-centered foundation of the work itself. I unapologetically lean towards the latter!

In our work in Akoben, these ideas are front and center for us. We've found our place on the battlefield where we are able to:

- center our Restorative Practices trainings within the social justice movement, which informs our understanding of power, privilege, and bias.

- explicitly connect Restorative Practices to trauma-informed care, cultural relevancy, and a strengths-based approach.

- use a wide cache of cultural examples, both historic and contemporary, that highlight how this work can be implemented in underrepresented communities.

- broaden this work so that it is approachable by everyone, including the "non-professionals", lay people, and youth.

We have designed workshops that bring these concepts to life, including "Developing a Restorative and Strengths-Based Approach," "Circles: A Powerful Way to Connect and Heal," and "Being the Leader We Need." You can learn more about Akoben at www.akobenllc.org.

The Call

We took our name, "Akoben," from the ancient Adinkra symbol for a war horn. The war horn would be used to call the community to come out and serve, to struggle for the good of the community. Our schools, organizations, communities, and families need Restorative Practices now more than ever. Can you hear the sound of the war horn? It's calling you to come out and start your own Restorative Journey.

Leading in the
Struggle to Serve

References and Resources

Block, P. (2018). Community: *The Structure of Belonging.* Berrett-Koehler, Incorporated.

Bond, B., & Exley, Z. (2016). *Rules for revolutionaries: How big organizing can change everything.* White River Junction, VT: Chelsea Green Publishing.

Boyes-Watson, C. (2008). *Peacemaking circles & urban youth: Bringing justice home.* St. Paul, MN: Living Justice Press.

Braithwaite, J. (2007). *Crime, shame, and reintegration.* New York: Cambridge University Press.

Costello, B., Wachtel, J., & Wachtel, T. (2009). *The restorative practices handbook: For teachers, disciplinarians and administrators.* Bethlehem, PA: International Institute for Restorative Practices.

Covey, S. R. (2016). *The 7 habits of highly effective people.* Selangor: PTS Publishing House.

Discipline Disparities for Black Students, Boys, and Students with Disabilities (Rep.). (2018, March). Retrieved https://www.gao.gov/assets/700/690828.pdf

Fitzgerald, M. F. (2006). *Corporate circles: Transforming conflict and building trusting teams.* Vancouver: Quinn Pub.

Hadley, M. (2001). *The spiritual roots of restorative justice.* Albany, NY: State University of New York Press.

Hattie, J. (2010). *Visible learning: A synthesis of over 800 meta-analyses relating to achievement.* London: Routledge.

Jensen, E. (2013). *Engaging students with poverty in mind: Practical strategies for raising achievement.* Alexandria, VA: ASCD.

Johnstone, G. (2011). *Restorative justice: Ideas, values debates.* 2nd. ed.-London: Routledge.

Lewis, S. (2009). Improving School Climate: Findings from Schools Implementing Restorative Practices. Retrieved from https://www.iirp.edu/pdf/IIRP-Improving-School-Climate-2009.pdf

Maruna, S. (2005). Shame, Shaming and Restorative Justice: A Critical Appraisal. In D.   Sullivan, & L. Tifft (Eds.), *Handbook of Restorative Justice* (pp. 452-462). Taylor and Francis

McLaughlin, E. (2003). *Critical issues in restorative justice.* London: SAGE.

Miller, C. C. (2016, March 18). As Women take over a Male Dominated Field, Pay Drops. *The New York Times.*

Nathanson, D. L. (1994). *Shame and pride: Affect, sex and the birth of self.* W.W. Norton.

Parrett, M. (2015). Beauty and the feast: Examining the effect of beauty on earnings using restaurant tipping data. *Journal of Economic Psychology, 49,* 34-46. doi:10.1016/j.joep.2015.04.002

Pfeiffer, R. H. (2005). *Real solution anger management workbook.* New York: Growth Pub.

Pranis, K. (2005). *The little book of circle processes: A new/old approach to peacemaking.* Intercourse, PA: Good Books.

Roy, S. (1986). *Cambridge English dictionary*. New Delhi: Pankaj.

Strong, H., & Sherman, L. (2007). Restorative Justice: The Evidence. *The Smith Institute.*

TEDTalks: Brene Brown--The Power of Vulnerability [Video file]. (n.d.).

Wachtel, T., O'Connell, T., & Wachtel, B. (2010). *Restorative justice conferencing: Real justice and the Conferencing handbook.* Bethlehem, PA: International Institute for Restorative Practices.

Watlington, Christina. Dr. Watlington & Associates at www. drwatlington.com

Zehr, H. (2002). *The little book of restorative justice.* Intercourse, PA: Good Books.

Acknowledgements

Asante Sana (Thank you very much in Swahili):

To my champion, partner in all things, confidant, greatest cheerleader and wife, Dr. Christina Watlington. Your love has embodied the power of challenge and connection to help change me into who I am. Truly, this work is because you believed that I had something to contribute.

To Ngozi for holding my hand throughout this journey. You led at times and I followed, you organized when I was scattered. You were the first published author in our family and your love, creative guidance and support were invaluable. Check out Ngozi Magena's powerful work: Sin and Virtue: A Collection of Poems. I'm the proudest Baba!

To Sadiki for inspiring me to be a better leader, if only to make you proud. I can't wait to see you smile when you read this book. Magical!

To my editor, Kara Garbe Balcerzak, and book designer, John Irvine, for your brilliant feedback and support. This work is so much better because of your creative approaches and support.

To Steve "Judge" Hornsby for introducing me to the idea of Restorative Practices and to Ted Wachtel and the International Institute for Restorative Practices (IIRP) for your leadership and my training in the field. I hope that I have made a small contribution here to the practices you have championed for so long.

To my brother Steve Korr who has done more to encourage, challenge and sharpen my Restorative Practices than anyone else. You are more of a leader to me than you will ever know.

To Patricia Harris for your encouragement, laughter, organization and prayers. I've needed them all.

To my mentors and encouragers: Warren, Govindh, Yasser, Liz, David, Coley, Tony and Dad. I heard and understand you, and this book is a commitment kept.

To my colleagues in our alternative schools and programs in Delaware. It has been an honor to learn and serve these beautiful young people together. The story of our victories and achievements hasn't been told yet.

To our Akoben Tribe for answering the call to come out and serve the community. I am honored to be on this part of the battlefield with you!

Finally, to those whom I didn't name, please blame it on my head and not my heart. Here is your chance to be acknowledged:

Thank you _____ for your _____.
        (print your name here)   (name your contribution)

About the Author

Dr. Abdul-Malik Muhammad is an organizer and activist for marginalized people, a leader and entrepreneur. He has spent over two decades serving youth and adults as a teacher, Principal, Campus President, State Director, Vice President and CEO. He is the founder of Akoben, a training and consulting organization and Transforming Lives Inc, a provider of alternative education services.

An acclaimed presenter, Dr. Muhammad speaks internationally on organizational, community and personal transformation through restorative practices, leadership and cultural relevancy. He holds a BA in International Affairs from Franklin & Marshall College, an MA in Educational Leadership from the College of Notre Dame of Maryland, and an Ed.D. in Educational Leadership from the University of Delaware.

He enjoys reading, refinishing wood furniture and traveling. He lives in Delaware with his wife, Christina, two young adult children, dad and wonderful dogs.

To find out more about Akoben, visit www.AkobenLLC.org or Transforming Lives Inc, visit www.tliservices.org.